NECESSARY SKILLS
FOR THE WORKFORCE

Housing & Safety

By Vivian Bernstein

CONSULTANTS

Dee Marie Boydstun
Literacy Coordinator
Black Hawk College
Moline, Illinois

Marie S. Olsen
Learning Center Coordinator
for Rio Salado Community College
at Maricopa Skill Center
Phoenix, Arizona

John C. Ritter
Teacher, Education Programs
Oregon Women's Correctional Center
Salem, Oregon

STECK-VAUGHN
BERRENT
A Harcourt Company

www.steck-vaughn.com

ABOUT THE AUTHOR

Vivian Bernstein is the author of *America's Story, World History and You, World Geography and You, American Government*, and *Decisions for Health*. She received her Master of Arts degree from New York University. Bernstein is active with professional organizations in social studies, education, and reading. She gives presentations to school faculties and professional groups about content area reading. Bernstein was a teacher in the New York City Public School System for a number of years.

CREDITS

Cover Photography: (smoke alarm) © Tony Freeman/PhotoEdit, (family moving & landlord with tenant) © Michael Newman/PhotoEdit
All photos by Park Street with the following exceptions.
p. 5 © Michael Newman/PhotoEdit; p. 6 © Richard Hutchings/PhotoEdit; p. 7 © Nicholas Sapieha/Stock Boston; p. 8 © Eric Neurath/Stock Boston; p. 9 © Lionel Delevingne/Stock Boston; p. 11 © Catherine Ursillo/Photo Researchers; p. 28 © Fredrick D. Bodin/Stock Boston; p. 29 © Tony Freeman/PhotoEdit; p. 32 © Robert Brenner/PhotoEdit; p. 48 © David M. Grossman/Photo Researchers; p. 51 © Robert Brenner/PhotoEdit; p. 58 © Barbara Rios/Photo Researchers; p. 59 © Judy Gelles/Stock Boston; p. 61 © Jose Carrillo/PhotoEdit; p. 68 © Tony Freeman/ PhotoEdit; p. 69 © Michael Weisbrot/Stock Boston; p. 70 © Tony Freeman/PhotoEdit; p. 72 © Tony Freeman/PhotoEdit; p. 80 © Eric R. Berndt/Unicorn; p. 82 © Amy C. Etra/PhotoEdit; p. 90 © Laima Druskis/Stock Boston; p. 91 © Bob Daemmrich/Stock Boston; p. 94 © Jan Lukas/Photo Researchers; p. 95 © Day Williams/Photo Researchers; p. 100 © Michael Newman/PhotoEdit; p. 101 © Anna Kaufman Moon/Stock Boston; p. 102 © Grant Leduc/Stock Boston; p. 110 © Barbara Rios/Photo Researchers; p. 111 © Bob Krueger/ Photo Researchers; p. 113 © Mark Richards/PhotoEdit.

Rental application reproduced with permission of E-Z Legal Forms.
Bleach label reproduced with permission of Topco Associates, Inc.
Ammonia label reproduced with permission of The Dial Corporation.
Warranty reproduced with permission of the General Electric Corporation.
Emergency information chart reproduced courtesy of the American Red Cross.
Benadryl warning label reproduced with permission of Warner-Lambert Company.
Paint warning label reproduced with permission of The Glidden Company.

We would like to express our appreciation to all local, state, and national governmental agencies that helped in the preparation of this book. In particular, we would like to thank the following for providing information and forms for the workshops:

Vital Records Office, Arkansas Department of Health
California Secretary of State's Office

ISBN 0–8172–6382–9

Printed in the United States of America.

3 4 5 6 7 8 9   073   11 10 09 08 07 06 05

CONTENTS

TO THE LEARNER

Necessary Skills for the Workforce: Housing & Safety can help you learn skills to be successful in your daily life and will show you how to use these skills. Each chapter in this book includes a lesson followed by a workshop and exercises. One workshop in this book is "Reading the Classified Ads." What kind of classified ads have you read before?

_____

_____

_____

In the "Thinking and Writing" exercise, you will be asked to write in your journal. Your journal can be a notebook or just a group of papers. Writing in a journal helps you gather your thoughts and put them on paper. One exercise in this book asks you to think about advice you would give a friend about finding a place to live. Thinking and writing about problems can help you find answers. Try it here. Think about questions or problems you may have about setting up your own home. On the lines below, tell how you think this book will help you.

_____

_____

_____

There are an index, a glossary, and an answer key in the back of this book. These features can help you use this book independently.

Have fun working through this book. Then enjoy your new skills!

CHAPTER 1

DIFFERENT KINDS OF HOUSING

THINK ABOUT AS YOU READ

- What are the differences between renting and buying a home?
- What kinds of apartments can you rent?
- How does the government help some people pay rent?

Tony Smith is looking for a new place to live. He has a good job. He has been saving part of each paycheck. Tony knows there are many places to live. He could try to buy a home. Or he could rent a home. Tony needs to decide what kind of housing he wants. He needs to find **housing** that he can afford. In this chapter you will learn about different kinds of housing.

The different kinds of homes people live in are called **housing**.

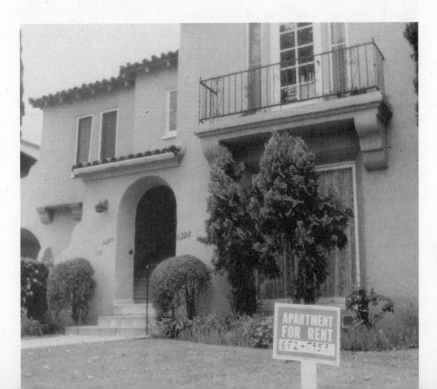

You have many choices in housing.

Owning or Renting a Home

Buying a home is expensive. Most people do not have enough money to pay for a home all at once. They borrow money from a bank to buy a home. This borrowed money is called a **mortgage.** Each month you pay back part of the mortgage to the bank. After you pay back all of the money, you will own your own home. It may take 25 or 30 years to pay off a mortgage.

To get a mortgage, you usually have to make a **down payment.** The down payment pays part of the cost of the home. The down payment is usually five to ten percent of the total cost. You may need thousands of dollars for the down payment. You may save money for several years to have enough for a down payment.

There are other reasons it can be expensive to own your own home. You have to pay for all of your home repairs. You have to pay **property taxes.** You have to pay for heating your home. You have to pay for the water that you use.

The money that you borrow in order to buy a house is called a **mortgage**. Mortgage money can be paid back over a period of many years.

A **down payment** is the money you pay in order to get a mortgage. The down payment pays part of the cost of a home.

Property taxes are the taxes you pay to the government on your home and your land.

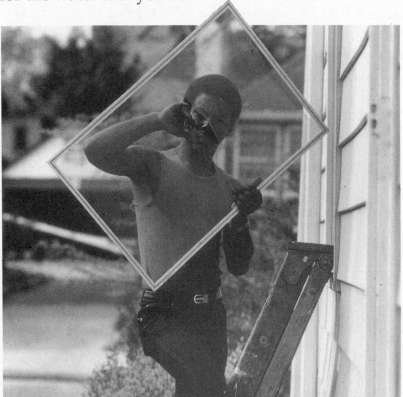

When you buy a home, you will have to take care of repairs.

When you rent a home, you will pay your **landlord** once a month. You will not need to make a down payment, but you will pay a **deposit.** Your landlord will want a deposit before you move in. The deposit may be equal to the rent for one, two, or three months. Before you move out, the landlord will walk through the home. If the place is in good order, your deposit will be returned. If it is dirty or in poor repair, the landlord will keep your deposit.

When you rent, your landlord may agree to pay some of your **utilities.** Your landlord may pay your water bills. Your landlord may pay for your heat and air conditioning. Usually the landlord will pay for repairs while you live there.

Different Kinds of Apartments

You may want to rent an apartment. Think about your needs before you look for an apartment. Where do you want to live? How much space do you need?

Your **landlord** is the person who owns your home and collects your rent.

A **deposit** is money that you give the landlord when you rent a home. The deposit shows that you plan to pay your rent each month.

Utilities are services to your home such as water, electricity, gas, and telephone.

You may find an apartment for rent in a house.

If you live alone, you may want to rent an **efficiency apartment.** An efficiency is one large room with a bathroom and a small kitchen. Or you may want to rent a room in a person's home. Your room may not have a kitchen or bathroom. You may have to share a kitchen and bathroom with other people in the house.

You may need an apartment with more space. Think about the number of bedrooms you will need. Decide if you can afford an apartment with one, two, or three bedrooms. Some apartments have more than one bathroom.

You may rent an apartment in a person's house. Some private homes are built with one or two apartments that can be rented. Your landlord will probably live in one of the other apartments.

You may decide to rent an apartment in an apartment house. Some apartment houses are part of a large group of tall buildings. Other apartments are in smaller apartment buildings. These buildings have fewer apartments. They have only one or two floors. You may have many choices when you look for an apartment to rent.

Other Kinds of Housing

You may want to rent a house. People with children often want to live in a house. A private house often has more rooms than an apartment. It may have a backyard.

If you have a **disability,** you may want to live in a group home. Group homes help disabled adults live on their own. Many group homes are private houses. About ten disabled adults live together in one home. The home will have **managers** to help you. During the day you will go to work. You will come back to the home at night. On weekends the managers plan activities for the members of the home. Most group homes have waiting lists. You may have to wait a few years until there is a room in a home for you.

You may feel that a group home would be a good place for you. Then call an office that helps the disabled in your community. Ask for information about these homes.

A **disability** is a problem that makes a person less able to do certain things. If you have a hearing disability, then you do not hear very well.

Managers are the people who take care of a group home.

Group homes help people live independently.

9

Looking for Housing

A good way to find housing is to look in the newspaper. **Classified ads** in the newspaper list housing for sale and for rent. These lists are placed in a separate section of the newspaper.

It takes practice to read and understand the classified ads. The Necessary Skills Workshop on pages 12 and 13 shows you how to read classified ads for housing.

Housing ads are listed under different headings. If you want to rent, look under "Rentals." If you want an apartment that has furniture, look under the heading "Furnished Apartments" or "Apts. – Furnished." If you want an apartment without furniture, look under the heading "Unfurnished Apartments" or "Apts. – Unfurnished." Some other headings are for condos and townhouses, houses for rent, and houses for sale. Sometimes ads are grouped by areas, towns, cities, or neighborhoods.

Most housing ads have a phone number to call. After you have found an ad that interests you, call the number. Set up a time to meet with the owner or landlord and look at the place. You may have to act quickly if it is a good deal.

You can also look around areas where you would like to live. Often there will be signs for housing for sale or for rent.

Paying for Housing

You can plan to spend one fourth of your **income** for rent. You may have to spend one third of your income for rent. You will not want to spend more than that for housing. You may also have to pay for your utilities. You need to decide how much you can afford to spend for housing.

You may want a roommate to help you pay the rent. A roommate can also share the cost of utilities. Choose your roommate carefully. You want a

Classified ads are ads in the newspaper for jobs, used products, and housing.

Your **income** is all the money you earn from your job and from interest on your savings.

roommate who will get along with you. You want someone who will help with the housework. You want someone who will pay a fair share of the bills.

The government may help you pay your rent if you have a low income. There are two ways the government may help you. The government may pay part of your rent in private housing. Under this program you will pay 30 percent of your income for rent. The government will pay your landlord the rest of your rent.

The government may allow you to live in public housing. The apartments in public housing are owned by the government. There is public housing for older adults and disabled adults. There are apartments for families with low incomes. Call the public housing office in your area to learn if the government can help you with your rent.

Think about the kind of home you want and can afford. Decide how many rooms you need. Decide how much money you can spend. Then you will be ready to go home hunting.

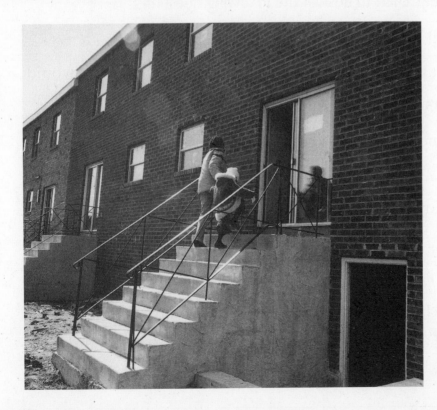

Public housing is provided by the government.

Reading the Classified Ads

Learning to use the classified ads may help you find housing. Many ads are written with abbreviations to save space. Use the abbreviations chart on page 13 to help you read and understand the ads.

Some ads say "All Bills Paid" or "All Utilities Paid." This means that the landlord will pay for gas, water, heat, and electricity.

Housing ads tell you the number of bedrooms and bathrooms in a home. The ad may say 2 br, 2 bth. The home has two bedrooms and two bathrooms. Or the ad may use numbers to show this information. An apartment with two bedrooms and two bathrooms will be shown as 2-2. A house with three bedrooms, two bathrooms, and a one-car garage will be shown as 3-2-1. An ad may say 1-1/2 for the bathrooms. This means that one bathroom has a bathtub or a shower and one does not.

■ ■ ■

Use the ads and the abbreviations chart to answer the following questions.

1. In ad #1, which bills will the landlord pay? _____

2. What kind of apartment is listed in ad #2? _____

3. Is the apartment in ad #3 furnished or unfurnished? _____

4. How many bedrooms and bathrooms does the apartment in ad #4 have?

_____

5. Which real estate company would you call to answer ad #7?

_____

6. The apartment in ad #8 is in what town? _____

7. Look at ad #10 and ad #11. Which of these two homes would you rather have? Tell why. If you would not like either of these homes, tell why not.

_____

_____

Apts. – Furnished

1. **Golden Oaks.** 1 bedroom. Exc location. Gas/elec paid. Nr stores, buses. $320 month. 874-2918

2. **Lakeview.** Efficiency. Tennis, pool. All bills paid. $385 month. 368-9400

3. **Redwood.** 2 br, 2 bth, new kit, W/W. Pool. $410. 576-3487

Apts. – Unfurnished

4. **Arlington.**
BRAND NEW!
HUGE 2-1
GAS PAID
Lndry. Microwave. Walk to railroad. $350. 462-1320

Apts. – Unfurnished

5. **Arlington.** Efficiency. W/W. Elev. Walk to shopping. $265. 899-0100

6. **Golden Oaks.** 2 bdrm, 1-1/2 bath, garden apt, new stove, refrig. $365. 674-9000

7. **Lakeview.** 1-1, 2-1, 3-2, W/D connections, new kit, d/wshr, huge rms. $350–$490.
Smith Realty 499-7300

8. **Redwood.** 1 bdrm, 1 bth, huge, near bus, 2 pools. $295. 794-5300

9. **Redwood.** Terrace Estates. 3-2, gar, pool, wsher/dry, gd loc. $515.
Wilson Realty 844-9009

Condos, Townhouses

10. **Arlington. Village Townhouses**, 3 bdrm, 1-1/2 bth, CA/CH, W/W, ABP, no dogs. $590. 675-1287

11. **Golden Oaks.** Twin Pines Townhouses 2-1, gas, new stove, refrig, microwave, W/D, W/W, pool, free cable, 5 minute walk to downtown. $590. 675-9843

Houses – Unfurnished

12. **Lakeview.** 3-2-2 home, new kit and baths, CA/CH, W/D connections, FP, large fenced yd, no pets, no smokers, new cpt. $875.
Wilson Realty 844-9009

Classified Ad Abbreviations			
ABP	all bills paid	**frig**	refrigerator
air cond	air conditioning	**gar**	garage
apt	apartment	**gd loc**	good location
br, bdrm, BR	bedroom	**inc**	included
bth	bathroom	**kit**	kitchen
CA	central air conditioning	**lge**	large
CH	central heat	**lndry**	laundry
cpt	carpeting	**LR**	living room
dep	deposit	**nr**	near
DR	dining room	**pk**	park
dry	dryer	**refrig**	refrigerator
dw, d/wshr	dishwasher	**req**	required
elec	electric, electricity	**rm**	room
elev	elevator	**W/D, wshr/dry**	washer/dryer
exc	excellent	**W/W**	wall-to-wall carpeting
fp, frpl, FP	fireplace	**yd**	yard

CHECK YOUR SKILLS

WORKSHOP PRACTICE: Use Ad Abbreviations

The ad on this page is for an apartment in the town of Lakeview. Use the abbreviations chart on page 13 to read this ad. Rewrite the ad using words instead of abbreviations.

Apt. – Unfurnished
Lakeview. Lge 3-2, DR, W/W, new cpt, d/wshr, new frig, W/D in kit, air cond, gas inc, gd loc nr bus, dep req. $490. 432-9926.

_____

_____

_____

_____

_____

_____

VOCABULARY: Find the Meaning

On the line write the word or phrase that best completes each sentence.

1. The money you borrow from a bank to buy a home is called a

   _____ .

         disability   mortgage   interest

2. Your _____ is all the money you receive from your job and from interest.

         down payment   utilities   income

3. When you rent an apartment, your landlord will probably ask for a

   _____ .

         deposit   interest   manager

4. Apartments that have one room are called _____ .

  utilities   efficiency apartments   landlords

5. People who own their own homes pay taxes for their home and land

called _____ taxes.

  property   income   housing

COMPREHENSION: True or False

Write True next to each sentence that is true. Write False next to each sentence that is false. There are two false sentences.

_____ **1.** You usually need a down payment to buy a house.

_____ **2.** You pay your landlord a mortgage when you rent a home.

_____ **3.** You do not have to pay for home repairs, electricity, water, and gas when you own your own home.

_____ **4.** You can plan to spend one fourth to one third of your income for rent.

_____ **5.** The government can help people with low incomes pay their rent.

On the lines that follow, rewrite the two false sentences to make them true.

_____

_____

_____

_____

Thinking and Writing

Look back at the classified ads on page 13. If you were looking for a place to rent, which one would you choose? If you would not choose one of these twelve homes, what kind of home would you like to have? Explain your answers in your journal.

CHAPTER 2

RENTING A HOME

THINK ABOUT AS YOU READ

- Where can you find information about apartments?
- What do you need to check when you look at apartments?
- What happens if you move out of your apartment before your lease ends?

Gina Garcia got a better job after she finished a job training course. She and her husband can afford to move to a new apartment. How can they find a new place to live? Where can they get information and help? What do they need to look for when they go apartment hunting? In this chapter you will learn how to find out about renting an apartment.

Check the newspaper for apartments for rent.

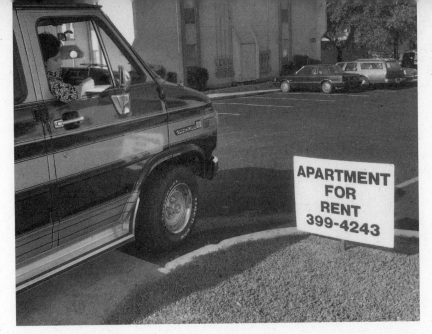

Look in an area you like for signs that apartments are for rent. Stop by or call the number.

Finding Out About Apartments

There are six places to get information about apartments.

1. Your family and friends may know about an apartment. Tell them you are planning to move.

2. **Bulletin boards** in stores, schools, community centers, and other public places sometimes have apartment information.

3. Sometimes signs outside apartment buildings say there are apartments for rent. There may be telephone numbers to call on these signs. Sometimes you can go into the building and speak to the **superintendent** or manager.

4. An apartment building may have a renting office. Call or visit a renting office.

5. Use the classified ads in a newspaper. Ads for apartments are listed under the heading "Rentals" or "Apartments for Rent." As soon as possible, visit apartments that interest you.

6. A **real estate agent** can help you find an apartment. Sometimes the agent will charge you a **fee.** Sometimes the landlord pays the fee.

Bulletin boards are boards on which ads and notices are hung.

A **superintendent** is a person who manages and cares for an apartment building.

A **real estate agent** is a person who sells and rents houses and apartments.

A **fee** is money that is charged for a service.

Check the apartment carefully. Make sure everything works correctly before you sign a lease.

Looking for an Apartment

Use the telephone to get information about places to rent. Perhaps you see an ad or a sign for an apartment. Call the phone number on the ad or sign. Ask about the rent, buses, and shopping. You may need to know if pets are allowed. Find out when the apartment will be **available.** If you think you will like the apartment, set up a meeting to see it.

Your appearance is important when you look at apartments. Your appearance shows the landlord that you will be a good **tenant.** Look clean and neat when you go to look at apartments.

Take time to look at an apartment carefully. Try to answer the following questions.

1. Are there enough rooms and closets?

2. Does the kitchen have a stove, an oven, and a refrigerator? Do they work? Are they clean?

3. Do the windows open and close easily? Do they have good locks?

4. Does the front door have a good lock?

5. Do the bathroom sink, toilet, and shower work?

6. Do the ceilings look like they have water leaks? Have the leaks been fixed?

An **available** apartment is one that can be rented.

A **tenant** is a person who pays rent to live in a house or an apartment.

7. Does the apartment have heating and air conditioning? Do they work?

8. Will my furniture fit in this apartment?

You will also want to check the neighborhood near the apartment. Walk around the blocks near the apartment. Think about whether you would like living in this neighborhood.

Check the building where you saw the apartment. Does the building look clean and safe? Are the lobby, halls, and elevator clean and well lit? Do the doors have good locks?

If you like the apartment, try to look at it a second time. If you saw the apartment during the day, try to see it again at night. You may want to take a friend or family member with you. Another person may notice something that you did not. Decide quickly if you want to rent the apartment. Another person may rent it if you wait too long.

Leases and Deposits

If you want to rent the apartment, the landlord will ask you questions. The landlord wants to be sure you will pay rent and take care of the apartment. You will be asked where you work. The landlord will want to know who will be living in the apartment with you. The landlord may want your Social Security number. The landlord may check your answers. Always tell the truth.

Some landlords refuse to rent apartments to people for unfair reasons. These unfair reasons are called **discrimination.** Discrimination is against the law. It is against the law to refuse to rent to people because of their race, religion, or sex. It is against the law to discriminate against people with disabilities. Call the human rights office in your state if a landlord refuses to rent to you for unfair reasons.

Discrimination means treating people unfairly because of their age, race, sex, religion, or disability.

A **lease** is a paper that a tenant signs when renting an apartment. A lease tells the amount of rent and the rules for living in the apartment.

To **renew** a lease means to get a new lease when the old lease ends.

Most landlords will ask you to sign a **lease** before you rent an apartment. Your lease will tell you what you can and cannot do with the apartment. The lease will say how much the deposit is. It will tell how much the rent is. It will tell what day of the month to pay rent. The lease will say how many people can live in the apartment. It will say whether pets are allowed. The lease will tell whether you or the landlord will pay for repairs.

The lease will say what the landlord will do for you. It will say if the landlord will pay for some of your utilities. It may say how to get your deposit returned when you move out.

Your lease allows you to live in the apartment for a certain period of time. Your landlord cannot raise your rent during the period of the lease. Usually you will not be asked to move if you pay your rent on time. Your landlord may ask you to move if you damage the apartment.

A lease usually runs for six months or one year. Some leases may run for two or three years. When your lease ends, you may want to **renew** it. Your landlord can raise your rent at that time.

Read the lease carefully before you sign it.

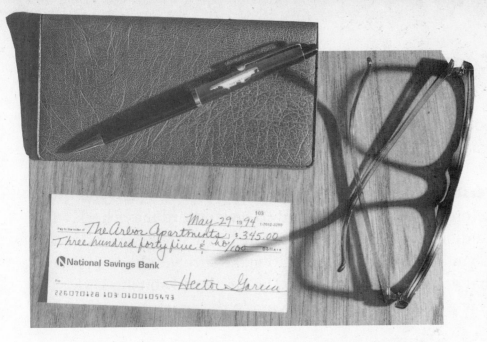

You may have to move before your lease ends. Moving out before the lease ends is called breaking the lease. If you break your lease, you may have to keep paying your rent until the lease ends. Write your landlord a note at least 30 days before you move out. The landlord may be able to rent your apartment to another person. Then you may not have to keep paying the rent.

You may decide to move out when your lease ends. If so, write your landlord a note at least 30 days before your lease ends. Tell that you plan to move. When you move, leave your apartment clean and in good repair. Then your landlord may return your deposit.

Do not sign a lease unless you understand it. Ask the landlord to explain anything you do not understand. Or you can ask a tenants' council in your area. Write on the lease if anything was dirty or broken when you moved in. Sign the lease if you agree with it. Keep a copy for yourself. Get a **receipt** for your deposit.

Sometimes it is hard to find an apartment. You may need to look at many apartments before you find the right one. Read your lease carefully before you sign it. Then you can begin moving into your new home.

A **receipt** is a paper that proves you gave money to someone to pay for something.

Completing a Rental Application

Look at the sample rental application on pages 23 and 24. It was filled out by Gina. Notice the following parts.

1 **Personal Information.** Your prior address is where you lived before the place you live now. The landlord may check with landlords you rented from before to see if you were a good tenant. The landlord wants to make sure you have a job so that you can pay your rent. The landlord wants to know how many people will be living in the apartment.

2 **Spouse Information.** The landlord wants to know if you are married. If your husband or wife has a job, then you may have help paying the rent.

3 **Bank Information.** The landlord wants to see if you have a bank account. Usually you will need to pay your rent with a check.

4 **Additional Personal References.** The landlord wants to check if you would be a good tenant. The landlord also wants a way to find you in case you do not pay your rent.

■■■

Use this part of Gina's application to answer the following questions.

1. Where does Gina live now? _____

2. How long has Gina lived at her current address? _____

3. What is the name of Gina's current landlord? _____

4. Where does Gina work? _____

5. How long has Gina's husband had his job? _____

6. What is Gina's checking account number? _____

RENTAL APPLICATION

1 PERSONAL INFORMATION

Date _May 20, 1994_ Interviewed by _Christine Herman_

Name of Applicant _Gina Garcia_ Telephone _449-0220_

Social Sec. No. _464-23-2986_ Driver's License No. _007-77-7777_

Present Address _413 Loyola Avenue_

City _New Orleans_ State _LA_ Zip Code _70112_

Prior Address _1020 St. Charles Avenue_

City _New Orleans_ State _LA_ Zip Code _70140_

How long have you lived at present address? _2 years_ How long have you lived at prior address? _1 year_

Name of Landlord _Carmen Sanchez_ Telephone _449-9600_

Prior Landlord _Mary Parks_ Telephone _432-7143_

Birth Date _April 19, 1949_ How many in your family? Adults _2_ Children _1_ Pets _1_

Employer _New Orleans General Hospital_ Position _Cafeteria worker_

How long? _3 years_ Telephone _624-4800_

2 SPOUSE INFORMATION

Name _Hector Garcia_ Birth Date _Feb. 3, 1948_

Social Sec. No. _109-87-7824_ Driver's License No. _008-88-8888_

Employer _Ramada Inn_ Position _maintenance worker_

How long? _2 years_ Telephone _624-3600_

3 BANK INFORMATION

Bank Name _National Savings Bank_ Telephone _374-8110_

Address _31 Poydras St._

Checking Account No. _0200306562_ Savings Account No. _12-382417_

4 ADDITIONAL PERSONAL REFERENCES

NAME	RELATIONSHIP	TELEPHONE
Dennis Kline	supervisor	624-4800, ext. 467
Mary Parks	prior landlord	432-7143
Mark Davis	minister	449-7462

5

OTHER INFORMATION

Number of vehicles (including Company Cars)____1____

Make/Model _Buick Skylark_ Year _91_ Color _white_ Tag No. _AAA 000_ State _LA_

Make/Model_____ Year_____ Color_____ Tag No._____ State_____

Make/Model_____ Year_____ Color_____ Tag No._____ State_____

HAVE YOU EVER

    Filed for bankruptcy? ☐ Yes ☑ No If yes, when?_____

    Been served an eviction notice or been asked to vacate a property you were renting? ☐ Yes ☑ No

    Willfully or intentionally refused to pay rent when due? ☐ Yes ☑ No If yes, when?_____

How were you referred to us?

☐ Newspaper (name)_____   ☐ Realtor (name)_____   ☑ Other _sign outside building_

Rental Unit applied for _970 Loyola Ave., Building 3, Apt. 5K_

Commencement date _June 1, 1994_ Term _2 years_ Rent/month _$345_

6

DISCLOSURE

I/(We), the undersigned, understand that _Christine Herman_ is the leasing agent and representative for the (owner)/landlord and that the leasing agent's fees will be paid by the (owner)/landlord. The undersigned acknowledge that this written notice was received prior to the undersigned receiving a lease agreement.

I/(We) declare the foregoing information is true and correct, and I/(We) hereby authorize you to conduct an employment and credit check and to verify our references.

Gina Garcia   5/20/94   _Hector Garcia_   5/20/94
Applicant's Signature   Date   Co-Applicant's Signature   Date

7

FOR OFFICE USE ONLY – DO NOT WRITE BELOW

Application Verification	Person Contacted	Remarks
☐ Present Landlord		
☐ Previous Landlord		
☐ Applicant's Employment		
☐ Co-Applicant's Employment		
☐ Bank		
☐ Reference (1)		
☐ Reference (2)		
☐ Reference (3)		
☐ Other		
☐ Driver's License/ID	☐ Credit Bureau	

Verification completed by_____

Date_____

Remarks_____
_____

	Monies Received	
Date	Description	Amount
	Applicant Fee	
	Deposit	

THIS APPLICATION
☐ Approved   ☐ Not Approved

5 **Other Information.** Some apartments have parking for their tenants. The landlord needs to know if you have a car. You may be given a parking sticker. The landlord also wants to know if you have had any rental trouble. The "commencement date" is the day the lease begins. The "term" is how long the lease lasts.

6 **Disclosure.** Fill in the landlord's name. Circle the word "we" if another person is renting the apartment with you. When you sign your name, you agree to let the landlord check the information you have given.

7 **For Office Use Only.** You do not fill in this part. But this lets you know that the landlord will be checking with your other landlords, employers, bank, and references.

■ ■ ■

Use this part of Gina's application to answer the following questions.

7. How many cars does Gina have? _____

8. What is her license plate number? _____

9. How did Gina find out about this apartment? _____

10. When does the lease begin? _____

11. How long is the lease? _____

12. What is the rent per month? _____

WORKSHOP PRACTICE: Complete a Rental Application

You may have to complete a rental application when you want to rent an apartment. Part of an application is on this page. Fill in the information. Use the form on pages 23 and 24 as a guide. You can use this sheet when you need to complete a rental application.

PERSONAL INFORMATION

Date_____ Interviewed by_____

Name of Applicant_____ Telephone_____

Social Sec. No._____ Driver's License No._____

Present Address_____

City _____ State_____ Zip Code_____

Prior Address_____

City _____ State_____ Zip Code_____

How long have you lived at present address?_____ How long have you lived at prior address?_____

Name of Landlord_____ Telephone_____

Prior Landlord_____ Telephone_____

Birth Date_____ How many in your family? Adults_____ Children _____ Pets_____

Employer_____ Position_____

How long?_____ Telephone_____

SPOUSE INFORMATION

Name_____ Birth Date_____

Social Sec. No._____ Driver's License No._____

Employer_____ Position_____

How long?_____ Telephone_____

BANK INFORMATION

Bank Name_____ Telephone_____

Address_____

Checking Account No._____ Savings Account No._____

ADDITIONAL PERSONAL REFERENCES

NAME	RELATIONSHIP	TELEPHONE
_____	_____	_____
_____	_____	_____

VOCABULARY: Matching

Match the word in Group B with a definition in Group A.
Write the letter of the correct answer on the line.

Group A   **Group B**

_____ 1. This means refusing to rent an apartment to   a. tenant
a person because of the person's age, race,
sex, religion, or disability.   b. lease

_____ 2. This person manages and cares for an   c. discrimination
apartment building.
                                                           d. superintendent
_____ 3. This person rents a home from a landlord.

_____ 4. This paper tells the amount of rent and the
rules for living in an apartment.

COMPREHENSION: Finish the Paragraph

Use the following words or phrases to finish the paragraph. Write the words
you choose on the correct lines.

tenant
clean
lease
landlord
safe
classified ads

You can get information about available apartments from
bulletin boards and the _____ in the
newspaper. Look at an apartment carefully before you rent
it. Make sure the apartment building looks
_____ and _____ . The
_____ will ask you questions before
renting the apartment to you. If the landlord feels you will
be a good _____ , you will be given a
_____ that tells how much rent you pay.

***Thinking and
Writing***

A friend needs to find a new place to live. What advice
would you give your friend about looking for a home?
Explain in your journal.

CHAPTER 3

Setting Up Your New Home

THINK ABOUT AS YOU READ

- What do you need to do to your apartment before you move into it?
- How do you get utilities for your apartment?
- What do you need in your apartment when you move?

Susan Jones rented an apartment. Susan wants to turn her apartment into a real home. There are many things she can do. In this chapter you will learn how to set up a new home.

Preparing Your Apartment

It feels good to move into a clean, freshly painted apartment. Your lease may say that your apartment will be cleaned and painted before you move into it.

Before you move in, you may want to paint your apartment.

Visit your apartment before your moving date. Check to see that your apartment has been cleaned and painted.

Sometimes a lease says the tenant will do the cleaning and painting. Then you may need to paint your apartment before your moving date. You may need to mop the floors and clean the kitchen.

After cleaning your apartment, think about how you want to cover your windows. Some apartments come with shades or blinds. Or you may need to buy them yourself. Measure your windows before buying window shades, blinds, or curtains. Take these measurements to the store. Buy shades, blinds, or curtains that will fit your windows. You can use sheets or towels until you find other window coverings.

Utilities for Your Apartment

Your apartment will need to have water and electricity. Your apartment may need gas also. You will need to make telephone calls. Arrange for utilities to be turned on before you move in. You may need to pay a deposit for some of your utilities.

You will need to know which utility companies to call. Sometimes your landlord will give you the names and telephone numbers of the utility companies. You can also learn this information from your neighbors.

To apply for electric service, call or visit your electric company. Do this about one week before you plan to move. You will need to give the complete address of your new apartment. Give the address and phone number of your job. Also give another telephone number where you can be reached. Tell the date you want electric service to begin.

Many landlords pay for gas and water for their tenants. Find out what utilities your landlord pays. Ask if you need to call the gas and water company to have service turned on.

Sometimes tenants pay for their gas and water themselves. Call your local water company about one week before you move. You will be asked your name, new address, telephone number, and **employment information.**

Employment information is information about where you work and the kind of job you do.

You will need to have your water and electricity turned on before you can get gas service. Sometimes a person from the gas company needs to visit your apartment to turn on the gas. The gas company will tell you which day a service person can come to your apartment. You will need to be there when the service person comes.

To start or change telephone service, call the business office of your telephone company. Tell your phone company when you want your service to start. You will be given a telephone number.

When you call the telephone company, you will be asked if you want any extra services, like call-waiting. Extra services add to the cost of your telephone bill. Start with just regular telephone service. You can order more services later if you really need them.

You can also choose a telephone company to handle your long-distance calls. Look for telephone companies in the Yellow Pages of your telephone book. Choose the company that will give you the best rates.

You may need to buy a phone. Buy a good phone. Cheap phones often break easily.

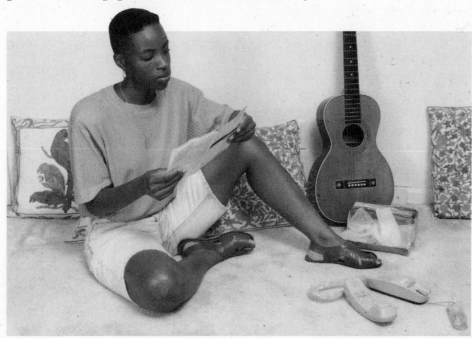

You can buy your own telephone to use.

Moving to Your Apartment

Before moving, pack most of your things in small boxes. Wrap dishes and glasses in newspaper so they will not break. Put them in boxes. Seal each box with tape. Mark on each box the room it goes in.

You may want to hire a moving company. Find a moving company that is honest and careful. Sometimes you can learn about a good mover from your family, friends, or neighbors.

Here is a list of things you need for your apartment on the day you move in.

1. light bulbs and a lamp

2. soap and toilet paper

3. food for dinner and breakfast

4. towels

5. a bed for each person

6. sheets, blanket, pillow, and pillowcase for each bed

7. a broom

8. a few chairs

Moving takes much planning and plenty of help.

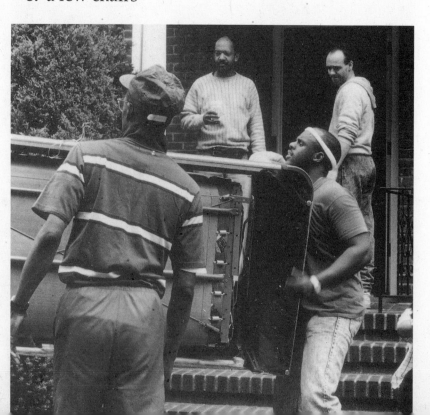

Turning an Apartment into a Home

You can make your apartment an **attractive** home. If you like plants, put some near your windows. You may have pictures to hang on your walls.

You may need to buy furniture for your apartment. Measure each room. Write down the room measurements. Think about how you will arrange furniture in each room.

Furniture can be expensive. Save money by buying furniture that is on sale. You can save more money by buying used furniture. You can find used furniture in **thrift shops.** Sometimes you can buy used furniture at yard sales and garage sales.

You can look for used furniture in the classified ads of your newspaper. Look under the heading "Used Furniture." Then look for the pieces you need. Call the telephone number in the ad if you find a piece you might want. Ask questions about size, price, color, and style. If you think you will like it, set up a time to see the furniture. Decide if you want to buy it only after you have seen it.

Your apartment may need **appliances.** It may come with a stove and a refrigerator. Or you may have to buy them. You may need a vacuum cleaner. You may want to buy a TV and a radio if you do not already have them. Save money by waiting for sales.

You can turn your empty apartment into a comfortable home. It may take money and work. When you are finished, you will feel right at home!

To be **attractive** means to look pretty or nice.

Thrift shops are stores where you can buy good used clothing and other products for a low price.

Appliances are machines that do certain jobs. A stove is an appliance that cooks food.

Completing a Change of Address Form

You will want to receive mail in your new home. If you complete a Change of Address form, the post office will send all of your mail to your new address. Letters that have your old address on them will be sent to your new home. You will need to complete a Change of Address form about one week before you move. Mail it to the city, state, and Zip Code of your old address.

Steven Eng completed a Change of Address form. Look at his form on page 35. Notice the following parts.

1 **Name.** Print your last name first. Put only one letter in each space.

2 **Old Mailing Address.** Put only one letter or number in each space. Leave a blank space between parts of your address.

3 **New Mailing Address.** You may need to look up your new Zip Code. The post office has a book of Zip Codes you can use.

■ ■ ■

Use Steven's Change of Address form to answer the following questions.

1. Is this change of address only for Steven or for his entire family? _____

2. When does Steven want his mail sent to his new address? _____

3. What is Steven's old address? Include his apartment, city, state, and Zip Code.

_____

_____

4. What is Steven's new address? Include his apartment, city, state, and Zip Code. _____

_____

5. Steven filled out this form how many days before moving? _____

INSTRUCTIONS

INSTRUCTIONS: Complete Items 1 through 9 and the address on front of form. Please print, except for Item 8 which **requires your** signature.

1. Check only one block. If the entire family is moving from the old address, check entire family block. If a member of the family remains at the old address with the same last name, check individual move block and fill out a separate change of address order form for each person moving from the old household. If the move is for a business, check the block marked business. Family members with different last names must file separate forms.

2. Indicate the date which you want mail forwarding to begin.

3. If your move is **TEMPORARY** (you will be returning to your original household within twelve months) indicate the date to discontinue mail forwarding. If you fail to fill out this date, your mail will be treated as a permanent order and will continue to be forwarded.

4. Print **ONLY ONE** last name of person(s) moving to the same address. If person(s) with the same last name are moving from the same old address to different new addresses, use separate forms. If this is a business move, print name of business. If more than one business is moving, separate forms must be completed.

5. If you have checked individual in Item 1, print first name of individual moving. If you have checked family move, print first name of the head of household, and include middle name or initials if they are commonly used. If business move, leave this item blank.

6. Print complete **OLD** address. If your **OLD** address is a rural route (RR), include the box number in the designated space. The abbreviation RR/HCR No. stands for Rural Route/Highway Contract Route Number. If your **OLD** address includes an apartment number, please provide it.

7. Print complete **NEW** address. If your **NEW** address is a Rural Route, include the box number in the proper space. If your **NEW** address includes an apartment number, it is needed for accurate mail delivery.

8. This change of address order is not valid without your signature. See note on front of form.

9. *COMPLETE ADDRESS PORTION ON FRONT OF FORM With City, State, and ZIP of your OLD Address.*

Detach Before Mailing

U.S. Postal Service **CHANGE OF ADDRESS ORDER**	Customer Instructions: Complete Items 1 thru 9. Except Item 8, please PRINT all information including address on face of card.	OFFICIAL USE ONLY

1. Change of Address for *(Check one)* ☑ Individual   ☐ Entire Family   ☐ Business

Zone/Route ID No.

2. Start Date — Month `0 2` Day `1 0` Year `9 4`

3. If TEMPORARY address, print date to discontinue forwarding — Month Day Year

Date Entered on Form 3982
M M D D Y Y

4. Print Last Name or Name of Business *(If more than one, use separate Change of Address Order Form for each)*
`E N G`

Expiration Date
M M D D Y Y

5. Print First Name of Head of Household *(include Jr., Sr., etc.)*. Leave blank if the Change of Address Order is for a business.
`S T E V E N`

Clerk/Carrier Endorsement

6. Print OLD mailing address, number and street *(if Puerto Rico, include urbanization zone)*
`5 2   C E N T R A L   A V E N U E`

Apt./Suite No. `4 L`   P.O. Box No.   R.R/HCR No.   Rural Box/HCR Box No.

City `N A S H V I L L E`   State `T N`   ZIP Code `3 7 2 0 6 - `

7. Print NEW mailing address, number and street *(if Puerto Rico, include urbanization zone)*
`5 9 9   P O S T   R O A D`

Apt./Suite No. `2 B`   P.O. Box No.   R.R/HCR No.   Rural Box/HCR Box No.

City `R I C H M O N D`   State `V A`   ZIP Code `2 3 2 2 0 - `

8. Signature *(See conditions on reverse)*
Steven Eng

9. Date Signed — Month `0 2` Day `0 3` Year `9 4`

OFFICIAL USE ONLY

OFFICIAL USE ONLY

Verification Endorsement

WORKSHOP PRACTICE: Complete a Change of Address Form

Imagine that you will be moving in three weeks. Your new address will be 219 Miller Drive, Durham, NC 27703. Use your address and the new North Carolina address to complete the Change of Address form.

U.S. Postal Service **CHANGE OF ADDRESS ORDER**	Customer Instructions: Complete Items 1 thru 9. Except Item 8, please PRINT all information including address on face of card.	OFFICIAL USE ONLY

Zone/Route ID No.

1. Change of Address for *(Check one)*   ☐ Individual   ☐ Entire Family   ☐ Business

2. Start Date — Month / Day / Year

3. If TEMPORARY address, print date to discontinue forwarding — Month / Day / Year

Date Entered on Form 3982   M M D D Y Y

4. <u>Print</u> Last Name or Name of Business *(If more than one, use separate Change of Address Order Form for each)*

Expiration Date   M M D D Y Y

5. <u>Print</u> First Name of Head of Household *(include Jr., Sr., etc.)*. Leave blank if the Change of Address Order is for a business.

Clerk/Carrier Endorsement

6. <u>Print</u> **OLD** mailing address, number and street *(if Puerto Rico, include urbanization zone)*

Apt./Suite No.   P.O. Box No.   R.R/HCR No.   Rural Box/HCR Box No.

City   State   ZIP Code

7. <u>Print</u> **NEW** mailing address, number and street *(if Puerto Rico, include urbanization zone)*

Apt./Suite No.   P.O. Box No.   R.R/HCR No.   Rural Box/HCR Box No.

City   State   ZIP Code

8. Signature *(See conditions on reverse)*

9. Date Signed — Month / Day / Year

OFFICIAL USE ONLY

OFFICIAL USE ONLY

Verification Endorsement

COMPREHENSION: Write the Answer

Write one or more sentences to answer each question.

1. What may you need to do to your apartment before you move in?

   _____

2. What information will utility companies want from you before they will turn on your service?_____

   _____

3. What do you need in your apartment on the day you move in?

_____

_____

4. Where can you buy furniture for your apartment without spending a lot

of money? _____

_____

5. How can you turn your apartment into an attractive home? _____

_____

_____

_____

VOCABULARY: Writing with Vocabulary Words

Use five or more of the following words or phrases to write a paragraph that tells about setting up a home.

employment
  information
utilities
deposit
appliances
attractive
thrift shops
classified ads

_____

_____

_____

_____

_____

_____

_____

_____

Thinking and Writing

When setting up a home, you need to do some jobs before moving in. Other jobs can be done after you move. What jobs would you do before moving in? What jobs would you do after moving in? Explain your answers in your journal.

CHAPTER 4

SETTING UP YOUR KITCHEN

THINK ABOUT AS YOU READ

- What appliances do you need in your kitchen?
- What utensils will you need for cooking?
- What kinds of food will you want to have in your kitchen?

Luis Rodriguez moved into an apartment. Luis wants to eat good meals in his own home. There are many things Luis needs for his kitchen so he can prepare meals. He has to start from scratch to stock his kitchen with everything he needs. He needs pots, pans, and dishes, as well as food. In this chapter you will learn how to set up your kitchen.

Setting up your kitchen takes planning.

Appliances for Your Kitchen

Many apartments come with a stove, oven, and refrigerator. The oven and refrigerator both have **thermostats** to control the temperature. Check to see that the thermostats are working correctly. To check the oven, buy a small oven **thermometer.** Put it in your oven. Then turn your oven on to 350 degrees. After 15 minutes, your oven thermometer should be close to 350 degrees. If it is much more or less than that temperature, your thermostat needs to be fixed.

You may want to check your refrigerator's thermostat, too. Set your refrigerator and freezer at the correct settings. Wait a few hours. Then put a small weather thermometer in the freezer. After a few hours, the thermometer should be at 0 degrees. Then check the temperature inside your refrigerator. Set the thermometer inside the refrigerator. After a few hours, the temperature should be close to 40 degrees. If it is not, you may have to fix or adjust the thermostat.

A **thermostat** controls the temperature of an oven, freezer, or refrigerator.

A **thermometer** measures temperature.

You can find many items you need at thrift shops.

A **discount store** is a large store with low prices.

A **food processor** is a small appliance that can chop, grind, stir, and mix foods.

A **warranty** is a company's promise to repair or replace a product if it does not work right.

You will need to have your own small appliances. Think about what appliances you need. Think about what appliances you want and can afford. You can save money by shopping garage sales, thrift shops, and **discount stores.**

You may need to buy a toaster. Or you may decide to buy a toaster oven instead. If you like to drink coffee, you may want an electric coffee maker. If you bake cakes and cookies, you may want to buy an electric mixer. A **food processor** would help you chop and slice food quickly. A microwave oven can defrost and cook food quickly. It can warm up leftovers quickly, too.

Most new appliances come with a **warranty.** A warranty is a promise from the company that made the appliance. The company promises to repair or replace the appliance. The Necessary Skills Workshop on pages 44 and 45 is about reading a warranty.

Pots and Dishes for Your Kitchen

Every kitchen needs pots and pans. Try to buy pots that can be used in many ways. Buy a lid for each pot. You will probably also need pans for baking.

Some pots can be used in the oven and on top of the stove. Many pots cannot be used in the oven. The heat from the oven will crack their handles. Other pots can be used in the oven but are not safe for cooking on top of the stove. All new pots have labels that tell you how you can use them. Read these labels carefully. Sometimes you can find good pots at garage sales and thrift shops.

You may want some of your pots to have a **non-stick coating** on the inside. A non-stick coating helps you cook meals with less fat. Most foods will not stick to these pots.

You will also need dishes. You will need large plates, small plates, small bowls, cups, glasses, and **flatware.** You will want to buy extra glasses, dishes, and flatware for when you have guests.

Utensils for Your Kitchen

You need many different kinds of **utensils** to prepare food. Make a list of the utensils you think you will need and use. Watch for garage sales. Shop around at thrift shops and discount stores. Take your list with you when you shop for your utensils.

The inside of a pot with **non-stick coating** has a special seal to keep food from sticking.

Forks, knives, and spoons are **flatware**.

Utensils are tools used for preparing and storing food.

When you have set up your kitchen, you can enjoy home-cooked meals.

KITCHEN UTENSILS

Use this list to help you stock your kitchen. Put a check mark by the utensils you have. Cross out the ones you do not need. Add more that you do need. Then take this list with you when you go shopping at garage sales, thrift shops, and discount stores.

_____ can opener	_____ microwave dishes	_____ drain rack or dish
_____ measuring cup	_____ potholders	drainer
_____ measuring spoons	_____ cookie sheet	_____ plastic containers for
_____ mixing bowls	_____ grater	leftovers
_____ large spoons	_____ vegetable peeler	_____ _____
_____ butcher knife	_____ vegetable steamer	_____ _____
_____ paring knife	_____ colander	_____ _____
_____ large fork	_____ timer	_____ _____
_____ cutting board	_____ rolling pin	_____ _____

Food for Your Home

Keep a supply of food in your home. Canned fruits and vegetables can be kept a long time. You can also keep cans of tuna fish for a long time. Cereals can last for a few months.

Other foods must be bought often. Cook fresh meat and chicken within two days. Fresh fish can last one or two days in your refrigerator. You can keep these foods for a few months if you put them in your freezer. Always wrap food in foil or in plastic before putting it in the freezer. This will protect it from freezer burn.

Buy fresh fruits and vegetables every week. You will need to buy fresh milk once a week. These foods can be kept for about one week in the refrigerator.

You may want to keep a supply of frozen food in your freezer. Frozen vegetables can be used instead of fresh ones. Frozen orange juice makes a healthy drink. You can store bread in your freezer. Take out a few slices when you need them.

You can learn to cook healthy, delicious meals. You will save money by cooking your own food. Ask your friends for easy **recipes** that they enjoy. You can also find good recipes in newspapers, magazines, and cookbooks from the library.

Recipes are directions for cooking or baking foods.

Keeping the Kitchen Clean

Always clean your kitchen after cooking. Scrub all pots and utensils. Make sure your sink and counter are clean. Clean your oven and refrigerator whenever they look dirty.

The freezers of some refrigerators have to be defrosted. Ice builds up on the walls of these freezers. When the ice gets too thick, the freezer no longer keeps food cold enough. Defrost your freezer when the ice is one fourth of an inch thick.

Never try to chip away ice that has built up in your freezer. You could put a hole in the freezer wall. That would ruin the freezer.

To defrost your freezer, turn your freezer off. Remove all foods and put them in an ice chest or wrap them in newspapers to keep them cold. As the ice in the freezer melts, it will drip into a pan below the freezer. As the pan fills up, pour the water into your sink. When all of the ice has melted, clean the freezer. Put the food back. Turn the freezer on again.

Your oven also needs to be cleaned. Try not to let your oven get too dirty. A very dirty oven is hard to clean. It does not cook food evenly. It can be unsafe. Wipe up spilled food in your oven when the oven is cool. Scrub your oven with a cleanser and steel wool. Rinse it with clean water. Dry it with a clean rag or towel.

Setting up your kitchen is a big job. It takes time and money to buy appliances, utensils, and food. It also takes practice to learn how to cook. You will enjoy eating good meals in your own home and having friends over for dinner.

Reading a Warranty

When you buy a new appliance, it usually comes with a warranty. A warranty can be a full warranty or a limited warranty. A full warranty promises to give you free parts and repairs for a certain period of time. The company might also replace the product if it cannot be fixed. A limited warranty only promises to replace certain parts for a certain period of time. A warranty never protects products that have problems because they were used carelessly.

A warranty tells you four things. It tells you how long the warranty will last. It tells you where you can get the product fixed. It tells you what kinds of problems the warranty does not cover. It tells you what to do to get the appliance fixed.

Always read the warranty to find out what is covered. Keep the warranty in a safe place. Always keep your sales receipt with the warranty. It shows the date you bought the appliance.

Look at the sample warranty on page 45. It is for a microwave oven. Notice the following parts.

 What Is Covered. This tells you what the warranty covers and for how long. A "manufacturing defect" is a problem caused when the appliance was made. A defect is the fault of the company that made it.

 What Is Not Covered. This lists the problems not covered by the warranty. To use this oven commercially would be to use it to make food to sell to the public.

Use the warranty to answer the following questions.

1. Is this a full warranty or a limited warranty? _____

2. How long is this product under warranty? _____

3. When does the warranty period begin? _____

4. What is not covered under this warranty? _____

_____

WARRANTY

Save proof of original purchase date such as your sales slip or canceled check to establish warranty period.

1 WHAT IS COVERED

LIMITED ONE-YEAR WARRANTY
For one year from date of original purchase, we will provide, free of charge, parts and service labor to repair or replace *any part of the microwave oven* that fails because of a manufacturing defect.

LIMITED ADDITIONAL FOUR-YEAR WARRANTY
For the second through fifth year from date of original purchase, we will provide, free of charge, a replacement *magnetron tube* if the magnetron tube fails because of a manufacturing defect. You pay for service labor charges.

For each of the above warranties:
To avoid any trip charges, you must take the microwave oven to a General Electric Factory Service Center or a General Electric Customer Care® servicer and pick it up following service. In-home service is also available, but you must pay for the service technician's travel costs to your home.

This warranty is extended to the original purchaser and any succeeding owner for products purchased for ordinary home use in the 48 mainland states, Alaska, Hawaii and Washington, D.C.

All warranty service will be provided by our Factory Service Centers or by our authorized Customer Care® servicers during normal working hours.

Look in the White or Yellow Pages of your telephone directory for GENERAL ELECTRIC COMPANY, GENERAL ELECTRIC FACTORY SERVICE, GENERAL ELECTRIC-HOTPOINT FACTORY SERVICE or GENERAL ELECTRIC CUSTOMER CARE® SERVICE.

2 WHAT IS NOT COVERED

• Service trips to your home to teach you how to use the product.
Read your Use and Care material.
If you then have any questions about operating the product, please contact your dealer or our Consumer Affairs office at the address below, or call, toll free:
The GE Answer Center®
800 626-2000
consumer information service

• Improper installation.
If you have an installation problem, contact your dealer or installer. You are responsible for providing adequate electrical, exhausting and other connecting facilities.

• Replacement of house fuses or resetting of circuit breakers.

• Failure of the product if it is used for other than its intended purpose or used commercially.

• Damage to product caused by accident, fire, floods or acts of God.

WARRANTOR IS *NOT* RESPONSIBLE FOR CONSEQUENTIAL DAMAGES.

Some states do not allow the exclusion or limitation of incidental or consequential damages, so the above limitation or exclusion may not apply to you. This warranty gives you specific legal rights, and you may also have other rights which vary from state to state. To know what your legal rights are in your state, consult your local or state consumer affairs office or your state's Attorney General.

Warrantor: General Electric Company

If further help is needed concerning this warranty, write:
Manager—Consumer Affairs, General Electric Company, Appliance Park, Louisville, KY 40225

CHECK YOUR SKILLS

WORKSHOP PRACTICE: Read a Warranty

Read the warranty on page 45 again. Imagine that it is for an appliance that you bought. Imagine that the appliance quit working after six months. You did not misuse it. Write a paragraph to explain what you would do to get the appliance fixed.

_____

_____

_____

_____

_____

_____

_____

COMPREHENSION: Circle the Answer

Draw a circle around the correct answer.

1. What can you use to check the temperature of your oven?

    thermometer

    freezer

    defroster

2. What appliance do you need if you want to bake cookies and cake?

    coffee maker

    toaster

    electric mixer

3. Why is it healthy to use pots with a non-stick coating?

    You can use less sugar.

    You can use less fat.

    You can use less salt.

4. How long can you keep fresh fish in your refrigerator?

one or two days

two weeks

two months

5. When do you need to clean spilled food in the oven?

as soon as the oven is hot

as soon as the oven is cool

once a month

VOCABULARY: Finish the Sentence

Choose one of the following words or phrases to complete each sentence.
Write the word or phrase on the correct line.

utensils
recipe
thermostat
warranty
flatware
food processor

1. A _____ controls the temperature in your oven.

2. A _____ is an appliance that can chop and grind foods.

3. Your _____ are the tools you use to prepare food.

4. When you buy an appliance, it usually comes with a _____ that promises that it will be repaired or replaced if it breaks.

5. Knives, forks, and spoons are called

_____ .

6. You follow a _____ to prepare a certain food.

Thinking and Writing

What appliances and utensils would you want when you set up a kitchen? Explain in your journal why you want each utensil.

CHAPTER 5

PLANNING HEALTHY MEALS

THINK ABOUT AS YOU READ

- What six nutrients does your body need?
- How can you plan healthy meals?
- How can you avoid getting food poisoning?

Matthew Johnson cares about having good health. He knows that eating the right foods will help him stay strong and fit. Now that Matthew is living in his own apartment, he wants to learn to prepare healthy meals. As you read this chapter, you will learn how to plan healthy meals. You will also learn safe ways to prepare food.

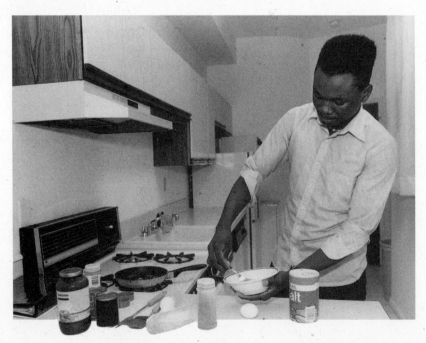

You can fix healthy meals for yourself.

Understanding Nutrients

Your body needs food in order to get **energy** and **nutrients.** Without energy from food, you cannot work or enjoy yourself. Without nutrients, your body cannot be healthy.

Your body needs six nutrients. You need **carbohydrates** for energy. Carbohydrates with **fiber** help the body remove wastes. You need **proteins** to build muscles, bones, and teeth. You need very small amounts of fat to keep your body warm. Fats also give you energy. Your body needs **vitamins** and **minerals** to work well. It also needs water to remove wastes from the body. Water helps keep your body at the right temperature.

The chart below shows some of the foods you can eat to get the nutrients you need.

Six Nutrients Your Body Needs					
Carbohydrates	Proteins	Fats	Vitamins	Minerals	Water
cereals	meat	butter	fruits	red meat	water
fruits	chicken	margarine	vegetables	beans	juice
vegetables	fish	peanut butter	cereals	milk	milk
bread	beans	cooking oils	rice	green vegetables	
rice	milk	whole milk	milk	fruits	
pasta	cheese				

Planning Healthy Meals

Your body needs two to three teaspoons of fat each day. Too much fat can harm your body. Foods that are high in fat can cause **cholesterol** to build up in the blood. Too much cholesterol can cause heart disease. So you need to plan a diet that is low in fat.

Energy is the strength to do things.

Nutrients are substances in food that the body needs for health and life. The six nutrients you need are carbohydrates, proteins, fats, vitamins, minerals, and water.

Carbohydrates A nutrient that gives the body energy.

Fiber is a carbohydrate from plants that helps the body remove wastes.

Proteins are nutrients that the body uses for growth and repair.

Vitamins are a group of nutrients that the body needs in small amounts in order to work and grow well.

Minerals are nutrients that are needed by the body to provide healthy teeth, muscles, bones, and blood cells.

Cholesterol is a fatty substance in the blood. Too much cholesterol in the blood can cause heart disease.

A healthy diet is low in salt and sugar, too. It is filled with fresh fruits, vegetables, and grains. These foods provide healthy carbohydrates and fiber.

There are many ways to limit the fat in your diet. Avoid eating fried foods. Choose a baked potato instead of French fries. Put nonfat yogurt on your baked potato instead of sour cream. Remove all chicken skin from your chicken. Eat broiled or baked chicken without skin instead of fried chicken. Buy cheese and mayonnaise that are low in fat. Use low-fat salad dressing. Avoid eating egg yolks. They are high in cholesterol.

Learn to eat low-fat snacks, too. Eat salt-free pretzels instead of potato chips. Try nonfat cookies and cakes instead of donuts and chocolate bars. Eat fresh fruit instead of candy and chips. Buy nonfat frozen yogurt instead of ice cream.

The Food Triangle can help you plan healthy meals. Plan to eat more of the foods listed at the bottom of the triangle. Plan to eat less of the foods at the top of the triangle.

The Food Triangle

Use very small amounts.
Fats, oils, and sweets

• **Fats and oils**
• **Sugars**

2–3 servings
Milk, yogurt, and cheese group

2–3 servings
Meat, poultry, fish, dry beans, eggs, and nuts group

3–5 servings
Vegetable group

2–4 servings
Fruit group

6–11 servings Bread, cereal, rice, and pasta group

The Food Triangle tells you how many servings from each food group you need every day. If you eat the right number of servings from each group, you will be getting the nutrients you need. By choosing low-fat food, you will be protecting your heart, too.

Matthew Johnson used the Food Triangle to plan his meals. He wanted to be sure he had enough servings from each group. He tried not to have too much fat, salt, or sugar in his meals. He also included healthy snacks. Look at Matthew's meal plans for two days on page 52.

Preparing Healthy Meals

It is not enough to plan healthy meals. You also need to use healthy ways to prepare your food.

Always start with clean hands. Wash with soap and water before you handle food. Use clean pots and utensils. After preparing food, wash all utensils and cutting boards with soap and hot water.

Try to prepare healthy, low-fat foods. Broil, bake, or boil foods instead of frying them. Cook vegetables for a short period of time in small amounts of water. Vegetables lose their vitamins when they are cooked for a long time.

When you fix healthy meals yourself, you can save money.

Matthew's Meal Plans

Day 1

Breakfast
glass of orange juice
slice of whole-wheat toast with
  margarine
slice of low-fat cheese
bowl of oatmeal
cup of coffee

Morning Snack
whole-wheat crackers
apple

Lunch
turkey and sliced tomatoes
  on 2 pieces of whole-wheat bread
green vegetable salad
  with fat-free dressing
banana
tea and water

Afternoon Snack
celery and carrot sticks

Dinner
1/2 grapefruit
whole-wheat roll
baked fish
brown rice
broccoli
lettuce and tomato salad
  with fat-free dressing
low-fat milk

Evening Snack
nonfat frozen yogurt

On Day 1, Matthew had
Milk group   3 servings
Meat group   2 servings
Vegetable group   5 servings
Fruit group   4 servings
Bread group   7 servings
He had only a small amount of
fat and sugar.
Matthew also drank 6–8 glasses
of water during the day.

Day 2

Breakfast
glass of grapefruit juice
2 slices of whole-wheat toast
  with margarine
scrambled egg whites
low-fat milk

Morning Snack
low-fat corn muffin with coffee

Lunch
low-fat cheese on a whole-wheat roll
  with lettuce and tomato
carrots
grapes
low-fat milk

Afternoon Snack
banana
granola bar

Dinner
bowl of vegetable soup
hamburger on a bun with
  lettuce and tomato
dill pickles
watermelon
tea

Evening Snack
salt-free popcorn without butter

On Day 2, Matthew had
Milk group   3 servings
Meat group   2 servings
Vegetable group   5 servings
Fruit group   4 servings
Bread group   7 servings
He had only a small amount of
fat and sugar.
Matthew also drank 6–8 glasses
of water during the day.

Each year many people get sick from food poisoning. Food poisoning can happen when food is not cooked for enough time. Cook eggs, fish, all meat, chicken, and turkey completely. Be sure the temperature inside your cooked food is high enough. The high temperature destroys germs that can cause food poisoning.

Many people get food poisoning because they do not handle raw **poultry** the right way. They do not wash their knives and cutting boards after they prepare chicken and turkey. Germs from the chicken and turkey are on their knives and cutting boards. When these utensils are used to prepare other foods, poultry germs become part of those foods. These poultry germs can cause food poisoning. You can protect yourself. Always rinse poultry before cooking. Pat it dry with a paper towel. After you finish preparing poultry, wash all the utensils with hot water and soap. Wash your hands, sink, and counter with soap and warm water.

You also need to use foods that are safe to eat. Look at canned foods before using them. Sometimes the cans are dented. Sometimes they are leaking, swollen, or rusty. Never use the food in these cans. You can get food poisoning from them. Throw these cans in the garbage or return them to the store where you bought them.

Check the **expiration dates** on foods. Many frozen foods, packaged foods, and foods in jars have expiration dates. Try to use foods before their expiration dates.

Be careful with other food, too. Fruits, vegetables, and bread become moldy as they age. Some molds are dangerous.

Planning healthy meals will help you get all the nutrients your body needs. Use healthy ways to prepare food. Avoid using food that may be spoiled. By eating healthy, well-cooked food, you will look and feel your best each day.

Poultry are birds like chickens, turkeys, and ducks that are used for food.

An **expiration date** is a date printed on a product. This is the last date a product should be bought or used.

Dividing Foods into Healthy and Less Healthy Choices

Your diet can help you have good health. Fresh fruits, vegetables, low-fat milk, and low-fat cheese are healthy foods. Lean meat, poultry, and fish are also healthy foods. Other foods can harm your health. Limit butter, fat, margarine, and fried foods. Avoid foods that have much sugar and salt. Avoid egg yolks since they are high in cholesterol.

Look at the foods listed below. Decide which foods are healthy choices. Write the names of the healthy foods under the heading **Very Healthy Choices.** Write the names of less healthy foods under the heading **Less Healthy Choices.** The first ones are done for you.

apple
bacon
banana
butter
candy bars
canned tuna in oil
canned tuna in water
carrot sticks
chocolate chip cookies
corn chips
donuts
egg yolks
French fries
fried chicken
fried foods
frosted cakes
fruit juice
grapes
hot dogs
ice cream

lean turkey breast
low-fat cheese
marshmallows
nonfat cakes and cookies
oatmeal
orange
plain baked potato
potato chips
salad
salami
salted peanuts
skim milk
skinless chicken breast
sour cream
steamed vegetables
sweet cereal
unbuttered popcorn
unsalted pretzels
watermelon
whole-wheat bread

Very Healthy Choices	**Less Healthy Choices**
1. _____apple_____	1. _____bacon_____
2. _____	2. _____
3. _____	3. _____
4. _____	4. _____
5. _____	5. _____
6. _____	6. _____
7. _____	7. _____
8. _____	8. _____
9. _____	9. _____
10. _____	10. _____
11. _____	11. _____
12. _____	12. _____
13. _____	13. _____
14. _____	14. _____
15. _____	15. _____
16. _____	16. _____
17. _____	17. _____
18. _____	18. _____
19. _____	19. _____
20. _____	20. _____

WORKSHOP PRACTICE: Plan Your Meals

Look at the Food Triangle on page 50. Use the triangle to plan your breakfast, lunch, dinner, and snacks for one day. Be sure to include enough servings from each group. Be sure to include 6 to 8 glasses of water.

Breakfast	Lunch	Dinner
_____	_____	_____
_____	_____	_____
_____	_____	_____
_____	_____	_____
_____	_____	_____

Morning Snack	Afternoon Snack	Evening Snack
_____	_____	_____

COMPREHENSION: Write the Answer

Write one or more sentences to answer each question.

1. What are the six nutrients your body needs?

_____

_____

2. Why do you need to avoid fatty foods?

_____

_____

3. Look at the Food Triangle on page 50. A healthy diet comes mostly from which three groups?

_____

_____

4. How can you avoid getting food poisoning? Write two ways.

_____

_____

5. What kinds of canned food can be dangerous?

_____

_____

VOCABULARY: Matching

Match the word or phrase in Group B with a definition in Group A.
Write the letter of the correct answer on the line.

Group A

Group B

_____ 1. These six different substances found in foods are needed by your body to work well.

a. cholesterol
b. expiration date
c. nutrients
d. fiber
e. poultry

_____ 2. Birds like chickens, turkeys, and ducks used for food are called this.

_____ 3. This fatty substance in the blood can damage your heart.

_____ 4. Do not buy or eat foods after this time.

_____ 5. This carbohydrate from plants helps the body remove wastes.

Thinking and Writing

Do you think the diet you are now eating is good for your health? Explain why. Tell what you can do to improve your diet. Explain your answers in your journal.

CHAPTER 6

CARING FOR YOUR HOME

THINK ABOUT AS YOU READ

- What products can you use to make your own cleansers?
- How often do you need to do different kinds of cleaning chores in your home?
- How can you keep pests out of your home?

Jackie Boyd is proud of her new apartment. She worked hard to clean it and paint it before moving in. Jackie wants to keep her apartment clean and in good condition. At the supermarket Jackie found many kinds of cleansers. She was not sure which ones she really needed. She was unsure about how to use them. In this chapter you will learn how to care for your home.

Kitchens usually have to be cleaned every day.

You will probably spend more time cleaning your kitchen than any other room.

Caring for Kitchens and Bathrooms

Kitchens and bathrooms need to be cleaned more often than any other rooms in the house. These rooms are used often. Germs grow on the sinks, counters, and toilets. Molds can grow in the shower and bathtub.

You will need cleansers for your kitchen and bathroom. You can buy cleaning products in the supermarket. Or you can make your own cleansers.

You may want to make your own cleansers. You will save money by making your own. The cleansers that you make are safer. They will have fewer poisons in them. They will cause much less **pollution** to the air and water.

What do you need to make your own cleaning products? You need white vinegar, **borax, baking soda, washing soda,** and water. You can also use some of the detergent you use to wash clothes to clean your kitchen and bathroom.

The chart on page 60 shows you how to use these supplies to clean your kitchen and bathroom. Wear rubber gloves to protect your hands when you are cleaning.

Dirt, chemicals, and wastes in the air and water cause **pollution**.

Borax is a white powder that is used for cleaning. Borax kills germs.

Baking soda is a white powder that is sometimes used for baking cakes and cookies. It is also used for cleaning. It kills odors.

Washing soda is a white powder that can be used for washing clothes. It can be used for cleaning floors, walls, and bathrooms.

Using Cleansers in Your Home

What to Clean	How to Make Cleanser	How to Use Cleanser
Bathroom Tub and Tiles	borax and water	Sprinkle borax on a damp sponge. Wipe tub and tiles. Rinse and wipe dry.
Toilets	1/4 cup borax	Put in toilet bowl. Wash bowl with toilet brush. Leave in bowl for 30 minutes. Flush toilet.
Windows and Mirrors	2 tablespoons vinegar 1 quart water	Put in spray bottle. Spray on glass and wipe off. Use paper towels, newspaper, or a clean soft rag.
Oven	Mix equal parts of salt, baking soda, and water.	Scrub oven well. Then be sure to remove all paste.
Freezer and Refrigerator	1/4 cup baking soda 1 quart warm water	Remove food from freezer and refrigerator. Dip sponge in baking soda and water. Wash inside freezer and refrigerator. Wipe with clean water. Then wipe dry.

A **poisonous** product or food is one that can cause a person to become very sick and perhaps die.

Ammonia is a liquid with a strong smell that is used for cleaning.

Chlorine bleach is a part of many cleansers. It is also used to make laundry whiter.

You may decide to buy some cleansers in the supermarket. Always read the labels and directions before using them. Many cleansers contain chemicals that are **poisonous.** Oven cleaners from the store can be very dangerous. They contain poisons. Wear rubber gloves if you decide to use them. Follow their directions carefully.

Never mix **ammonia** with **chlorine bleach.** When ammonia and chlorine bleach are mixed, they give off a dangerous gas. In the store you can find ammonia in cleansers for floors, walls, and windows. You can find chlorine bleach in products used for cleaning sinks, tiles, and clothing. Read the labels to learn if a cleaning product has ammonia or chlorine bleach.

The best way to care for your home is to keep it from getting very dirty. Wipe the top of your stove whenever food spills on it. Clean up spills on floors and counters right away. Wipe spills from your oven as soon as your oven is cool. Wipe your bathroom sink, tub, and tiles with cleansers to prevent soap, dirt, and molds from building up. Borax is a cleanser that kills germs. By cleaning with borax, you will kill the germs and molds that can grow in your bathroom and kitchen. Always rinse off cleansers with lots of clean water.

Cleaning Other Parts of Your Home

The other rooms in your house need cleaning, too. Clean the floors. Vacuum your rugs and carpets. You can wash tile floors, but wipe your wooden floors with a dust mop. Dust your furniture. Get rid of old newspapers and mail. You can give used clothing to thrift shops. Put clean sheets and pillowcases on the beds once a week.

You can do a few cleaning chores each day. You do not have to clean all parts of your home in one day. The chart on page 62 shows how often to do different kinds of cleaning chores in your home.

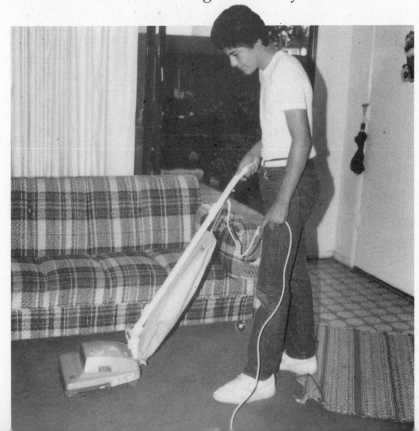

Try to vacuum once a week.

Cleaning Plan

How Often	Type of Chore
Every day	Clean kitchen counters and sink.
Once a week	Clean bathroom sink and toilet. Clean kitchen and bathroom floors. Vacuum carpets and rugs. Change bed sheets and pillowcases. Dust furniture.
Once a month	Clean inside of refrigerator. Clean inside of oven. Clean bathtub and shower tiles.
Once a year	Defrost freezer. Clean inside kitchen cabinets.

Plan when you want to do chores that need to be done once a month. You may decide to clean your refrigerator during the first week of the month. You can clean your oven during the second week of the month. It is easier to care for your home when you do not have too many chores at once.

Controlling Pests in Your Home

Insects and mice are pests that can enter a home. There are ways you can keep pests out of your home.

To keep mice out of your home, keep all food in closed jars and containers. Mice can get through very tiny holes and cracks. Have your landlord close all holes and cracks in your walls and floors. Check under your sink to see if there are openings in the walls near the pipes. You can fill these openings and cracks with steel wool.

If you have seen a mouse in your home, put mouse traps where you saw the mouse. Put a little peanut butter in each trap. The mouse will be caught when it tries to eat the peanut butter on the trap.

Some people use mouse poisons to get rid of mice. Mouse poison is placed in small cups. The mice die soon after they eat it. Be careful with mouse poisons. Keep them away from children and pets.

Sometimes people find cockroaches in their homes. Cockroaches carry many kinds of diseases. You can control these pests with a product called **boric acid.** You can buy it in a grocery store or hardware store. Sprinkle boric acid powder in your kitchen and bathroom along the cracks of your cabinets and floor. After a week or two, the cockroaches will be gone. Use this product carefully. It is poisonous to pets, children, and adults. Wear rubber gloves and a dust mask when you use boric acid. Follow all directions on the label.

You may want to buy an **insecticide** spray to kill cockroaches and other pests. Use insecticides carefully. They contain poisonous chemicals. Be careful not to use insecticides near food. Keep them away from children. Open the windows of the room where you spray. Always read the directions on the package before using an insecticide. Boric acid is a safer way to control cockroaches.

Flies also carry many kinds of diseases. Have your landlord put screens on all windows. The landlord may need to repair screens that have holes in them. Flies look for food. So keep food covered until you eat it. Cover all garbage pails tightly. Never eat food that flies have landed on.

After you set up your apartment, you will want to take care of it. You need to plan when to clean your home. Decide what kinds of cleansers to use. You will want to keep pests out of your home. Then you will be proud to call your apartment your home.

Boric acid is a poisonous powder that kills cockroaches. Sometimes it is colored so that you will not think it is baking soda.

An **insecticide** is a poisonous product that is used to kill insects. Many insecticides come in spray cans.

Reading Labels

It is very important to read labels on all cleaning products. Many dangerous chemicals are used in cleaning products. Read all labels to learn how to use products correctly.

Chlorine bleach is a common household product. Look at the bleach label on page 65. Notice the following parts.

1 **Laundering Directions.** These directions tell how much bleach to use when you are doing laundry, if you use bleach in your laundry. The directions give several measurements:

tbsp. = tablespoon

gal. = gallon

qt. = quart

To "dilute" means to mix the bleach with water before adding it to something else. These directions also tell you what type of clothes you cannot bleach safely.

2 **General Cleaning and Deodorization.** These directions tell you how to use bleach to get rid of dirt and odors. "Deodorization" is to remove odors.

3 **Caution.** This part tells you how dangerous bleach can be. It warns you not to get bleach on your skin or in your eyes. To "take internally" means to swallow it.

4 **First Aid Directions.** This part tells you what to do for problems. To "flush" with water means to wash off with plenty of water. To "induce vomiting" means to make someone throw up.

5 **Other Important Notice.** This part tells you not to mix bleach with any other household chemicals. It also tells you not to get bleach on food.

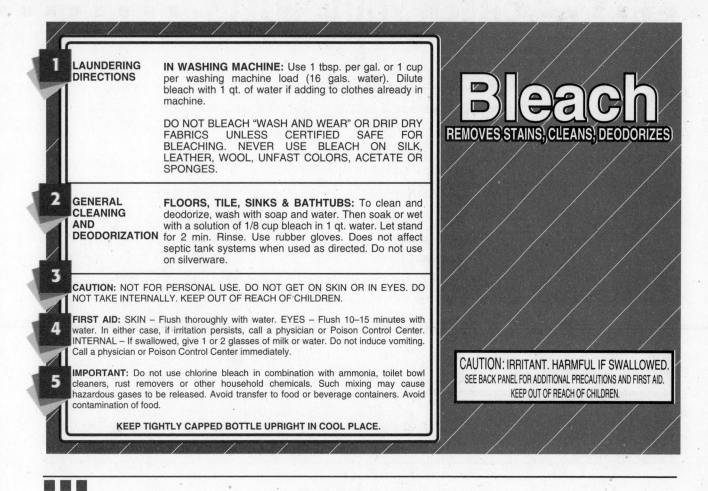

1 LAUNDERING DIRECTIONS

IN WASHING MACHINE: Use 1 tbsp. per gal. or 1 cup per washing machine load (16 gals. water). Dilute bleach with 1 qt. of water if adding to clothes already in machine.

DO NOT BLEACH "WASH AND WEAR" OR DRIP DRY FABRICS UNLESS CERTIFIED SAFE FOR BLEACHING. NEVER USE BLEACH ON SILK, LEATHER, WOOL, UNFAST COLORS, ACETATE OR SPONGES.

2 GENERAL CLEANING AND DEODORIZATION

FLOORS, TILE, SINKS & BATHTUBS: To clean and deodorize, wash with soap and water. Then soak or wet with a solution of 1/8 cup bleach in 1 qt. water. Let stand for 2 min. Rinse. Use rubber gloves. Does not affect septic tank systems when used as directed. Do not use on silverware.

3 CAUTION: NOT FOR PERSONAL USE. DO NOT GET ON SKIN OR IN EYES. DO NOT TAKE INTERNALLY. KEEP OUT OF REACH OF CHILDREN.

4 FIRST AID: SKIN – Flush thoroughly with water. EYES – Flush 10–15 minutes with water. In either case, if irritation persists, call a physician or Poison Control Center. INTERNAL – If swallowed, give 1 or 2 glasses of milk or water. Do not induce vomiting. Call a physician or Poison Control Center immediately.

5 IMPORTANT: Do not use chlorine bleach in combination with ammonia, toilet bowl cleaners, rust removers or other household chemicals. Such mixing may cause hazardous gases to be released. Avoid transfer to food or beverage containers. Avoid contamination of food.

KEEP TIGHTLY CAPPED BOTTLE UPRIGHT IN COOL PLACE.

Bleach
REMOVES STAINS, CLEANS, DEODORIZES)

CAUTION: IRRITANT. HARMFUL IF SWALLOWED. SEE BACK PANEL FOR ADDITIONAL PRECAUTIONS AND FIRST AID. KEEP OUT OF REACH OF CHILDREN.

Use the bleach label to answer the following questions.

1. If you put this bleach in your washing machine, how much would you use?

   _____

2. If the clothes are already in the washing machine, how do you add the bleach?

   _____

3. Should you use bleach on wool clothes? _____

4. How much bleach do you add to a quart of water to clean a bathtub? _____

5. Should you use bleach on silverware? _____

6. If someone swallows bleach, what should you do? _____

   _____

7. What does the label say may happen if bleach is mixed with other chemicals?

   _____

CHECK YOUR SKILLS

WORKSHOP PRACTICE: Read a Label

Look at the label below. It is for ammonia. Read it and answer the questions.

GENERAL CLEANING: 1/2 cup of ammonia per gallon of warm water cleans floors, walls, tile, woodwork, shower stalls — any large area in your kitchen or bathroom.

TOUGH JOBS: Use ammonia full strength to remove scuff marks and greasy fingerprints. Pour ammonia in your toilet, drain, or garbage disposal to keep them clean and odor free.

DO NOT USE TO SOAK ALUMINUM PANS.

CAUTION: DO NOT MIX WITH OTHER HOUSEHOLD PRODUCTS SUCH AS CHLORINE-TYPE BLEACHES, AUTOMATIC TOILET BOWL, WALL OR TILE CLEANERS. Avoid contact with eyes and prolonged contact with skin. Do not take internally. Avoid inhalation of vapors. Use in well-ventilated area.

KEEP OUT OF REACH OF CHILDREN.

FIRST AID:
EYES — Flush 10-15 minutes with water. Call a physician.
SKIN – Flush thoroughly with water.
INTERNAL – Immediately give large amounts of milk or water. Do not induce vomiting. Call a physician immediately.

AMMONIA
ALL-PURPOSE CLEANER

CAUTION: HARMFUL IF SWALLOWED.
IRRITANT. CAREFULLY READ PRECAUTIONS ON BACK.

1. How much ammonia do you mix with a gallon of water to clean floors?

   _____

2. Should you use ammonia on aluminum pans? _____

3. What does the label say to do if you get ammonia on your skin or in

   your eyes? _____

4. Would it be better to have the windows open or closed when you use

   ammonia? _____

VOCABULARY: Find the Meaning

On the line write the word or phrase that best completes each sentence.

1. A cleanser that makes laundry whiter is _____ .

   ammonia   chlorine bleach   insecticide

2. Dirt, chemicals, and wastes sent into the air and water cause

   _____ .

   pollution   boric acid   ammonia

3. A cleanser that is also used for baking cakes and cookies is

   _____ .

   boric acid　　washing soda　　baking soda

4. A powder that kills cockroaches is _____ .

   boric acid　　borax　　ammonia

5. Any product that can make you sick and cause death is

   _____ .

   safe　　poisonous　　cheap

COMPREHENSION: True or False

Write True next to each sentence that is true. Write False next to each sentence that is false. There are three false sentences.

_____ 1. Chemicals used in cleansers are not poisonous.

_____ 2. It is safe to mix ammonia with chlorine bleach.

_____ 3. You can clean mirrors and windows with water and white vinegar.

_____ 4. Borax is a cleanser that kills germs.

_____ 5. Mouse poisons and insecticides are safe for children, adults, and pets.

On the lines that follow, rewrite the three false sentences to make them true.

_____

_____

_____

Thinking and Writing

What are two good reasons for making your own cleansers? What are some good reasons for buying cleansers instead? Decide if you would like to make your own cleansers or buy them in a store. Explain your answers in your journal.

CHAPTER 7

HOME EMERGENCIES

THINK ABOUT AS YOU READ

- What emergency supplies do you need in your home?
- What do you need to know when you call 9–1–1?
- How can you handle emergencies?

An **emergency** is a dangerous time that needs to be handled quickly and correctly. Often outside help is needed to handle a home emergency.

Marta Díaz smelled gas in her home when she opened her door. She knew that this was dangerous. This was an **emergency.** She shut her door and went to her neighbor's house. Marta used her neighbor's phone to call the gas company. She waited at her neighbor's home until a service person from the gas company came to fix the leak.

A home emergency makes your home unsafe. Home emergencies can cause death. In this chapter you will learn what to do in a home emergency.

Always call the gas company to check for gas leaks.

Call for an ambulance if someone needs emergency medical help.

Handling Home Emergencies

Your home needs supplies for an emergency. Keep these emergency supplies in a closet that is easy to reach.

bottled water	first-aid kit
flashlight	blankets
battery radio	extra batteries
candles	matches
canned food	can opener (not electric)

Wherever you live, have a list of emergency numbers handy. The front of your phone book lists emergency numbers. In many cities and towns you can get emergency help by calling 9–1–1. Dial 9–1–1 to call the police or fire department in an emergency.

You can call 9–1–1 to get emergency medical help. Ask for an **ambulance** if a person is badly burned or badly hurt. Call for an ambulance if a person is **unconscious.** You need an ambulance if you think a person is having a heart attack.

An **ambulance** is a van that is used to take a sick or injured person to the hospital.

People are **unconscious** when they pass out or faint.

69

Check the battery in your smoke detector to be sure it is working.

An **operator** is a worker who answers the phone.

You can call 9–1–1 from a different place than the address where help is needed. You can dial 9-1-1 from a pay phone without paying. Follow these steps when you call 9–1–1.

1. Dial 9–1–1. An emergency **operator** will answer. Each operator has a number. You will be told your operator's number. Write down your operator's number.

2. The operator will ask, "What is your emergency?" State your emergency. You will be asked if you need a police officer, the fire department, or emergency medical care. You will be asked if you need an ambulance. Tell the operator what you need.

3. The operator will ask for your first and last name. You will be asked for the address where help is needed. State your full name. State the address and apartment number where help is needed.

4. Stay on the phone until the emergency operator tells you to hang up. Your call to 9–1–1 will be recorded.

Emergencies Caused by Fires

Have a **smoke detector** in your home. Check the battery in your smoke detector once a month. Put a new battery in the smoke detector when the old one no longer works.

You can prevent many home fires. Keep towels and paper away from the stove. Keep the stovetop and oven clean so grease does not catch on fire. Do not hang curtains close to the stove. Cigarettes cause many home fires, so be careful if you smoke.

Sometimes fires start in the kitchen. Food in a pot may catch on fire. Oil can catch on fire if it gets too hot. If this happens, turn off the stove. Do not pick up the pot or put water on the fire. Throw salt or baking soda on the fire. Then cover the burning pot with a lid. The fire will soon go out.

A fire can also start in your oven. If this happens, leave the food in the oven. Turn the oven off. Throw baking soda on the fire. Close the oven door. The fire will soon go out.

Keep a **fire extinguisher** on a wall where it is easy to reach. A fire extinguisher that has the letters ABC printed on it can put out all kinds of fires.

A **smoke detector** is a small machine that beeps when there is smoke in a room or hallway.

A **fire extinguisher** is a container filled with chemicals. When these chemicals are sprayed on a fire, the fire is put out.

Be prepared. Keep a fire extinguisher handy.

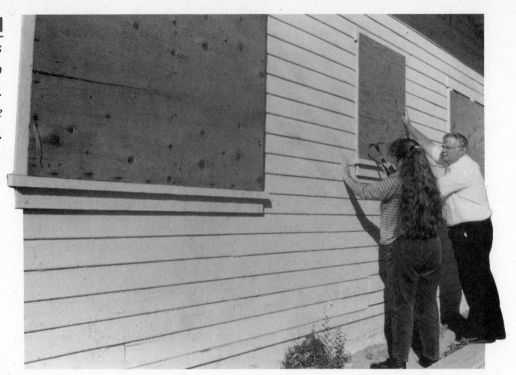

When a hurricane is coming, listen to weather reports. You will have time to prepare.

Plan how you can escape from your home during a fire. Practice your escape plan with everyone who lives in your home. Have a place to meet outside. If a fire starts in your home, use your escape plan to leave quickly. Never go back into a burning home after you have left. After you are out of the burning home, call the fire department or 9–1–1 from a neighbor's home.

Natural Disasters

Tornadoes, hurricanes, and floods are **natural disasters** that can damage your home. They can cause accidents and deaths. Weather reports warn you when tornadoes, hurricanes, and floods are coming.

Once you know there may be a hurricane or flood, try to make your home safer. Fill your tub and jars with emergency drinking water. Bring outdoor furniture indoors. To prepare for a hurricane, place wide strips of tape across all of your windows. The tape helps prevent glass from shattering. You can also board up windows.

A **tornado** is a kind of windstorm. It is shaped like a funnel.

A **hurricane** is a dangerous storm with heavy rains and strong winds.

A **natural disaster** is an accident caused by nature.

WORKSHOP PRACTICE: Complete an Emergency Chart

Complete the top part of the Emergency Information Chart. For "Other" you may want to write down the number for reporting a power failure or gas leak. Attach the chart to a wall near your phone. In an emergency the EMS operator will ask you to answer the questions in the lower half of the chart. Be ready to answer them.

Emergency Information Chart

Emergency Telephone Numbers

EMS_____ Fire_____

Poison Control Center _____ Police_____

Ambulance_____ Other_____

Family Physician: Name_____ Phone_____

Nearest Hospital: Name_____ Phone_____

           Address _____

_____

      Directions_____

_____

When you call EMS, be ready to provide the following information:

Your name _____

Type of emergency _____

Location of emergency _____
        street address

_____
        apartment number

_____
        nearby landmarks

_____
        major intersections

Telephone number you're calling from _____

How many are injured? _____

DON'T HANG UP UNTIL THE DISPATCHER TELLS YOU TO!

During a tornado try to stay in a basement. If you do not have a basement, wait in a hall, closet, bathtub, or room that has no windows or outside walls.

During dangerous storms listen to your radio. You may be told to **evacuate** your home. You will be told where to go for shelter.

Bad storms and hurricanes sometimes cause floods. If you think your house will be flooded, turn off the gas and electricity. Go to an upper floor if you can. Evacuate your home if you are told to do so.

Evacuate means to leave.

Gas Emergencies and Power Failures

If you ever smell gas while you are in your home, turn off your stove and appliances. Then do what Marta did. Call the gas company or 9–1–1 from a neighbor's home. Tell the gas company that you smell gas. Wait there until help arrives.

What happens if every light in your house suddenly goes out? Then you are having a **power failure.** During a power failure, turn off all electric lights. Turn off all appliances. Leave one light switch turned on so you will know when the electricity starts again. Use flashlights from your emergency supplies. Listen to your battery radio to learn what has happened.

During a **power failure** there is no electricity. All electric lights and appliances stop working.

Some power failures last a few days. In cold weather wear warm clothes to keep warm. Try not to open your freezer and refrigerator often. The food in your refrigerator will stay cold for at least one day if you do not open the door often.

You can learn to handle home emergencies. Prepare emergency supplies and put them in a place that is easy to reach. Learn how to call for emergency help. Listen to weather warnings so you can prepare for natural disasters. Work hard to prevent fires in your home. By doing these things, you will be able to handle many kinds of home emergencies.

Completing an Emergency Information Chart

Look at the Emergency Information Chart completed by Marta on page 75. Notice the following parts.

1 **Emergency Telephone Numbers.** During a home emergency, you may not have time to look for telephone numbers. You need to know the EMS number for your community. EMS means Emergency Medical Services. In many cities and towns, 9–1–1 is the EMS telephone number. Look in the front of your telephone book for emergency numbers.

2 **When You Call EMS.** The bottom part asks for information about your emergency. You will need to tell the EMS operator, or dispatcher, the kind of emergency and the address where help is needed. The telephone number you call from may be different from your home phone. Do not hang up until the dispatcher tells you to. The dispatcher may need to tell you what to do before help arrives.

■■■

Read the Emergency Information Chart filled out by Marta. Use the chart to answer these questions.

1. What is Marta's EMS telephone number? _____

2. What number can she call if someone is poisoned? _____

3. Marta is deaf. What is the Deaf Emergency number? _____

4. Who is Marta's doctor? _____

5. What is the closest hospital? _____

6. What is the phone number for the hospital? _____

7. What is the number to report a fire? _____

8. What is the number for the police? _____

Emergency Information Chart

1 **Emergency Telephone Numbers**

EMS ___911___ Fire ___753 – 6112___

Poison Control Center ___244 – 2000___ Police ___762 – 150___

Ambulance ___911___ Other ___Deaf TDD 1-800-34___

Family Physician: Name ___Dr. Alicia Smith___ Phone ___972 – ___

Nearest Hospital: Name ___Community Hospital___ Phone ___555 – ___

Address ___2445 Oceanside Rd.___
___Oceanside, NY   11572___

Directions ___Go east on Windsor Parkway t___
___Rd. Make a left turn on Ocea___
___Go straight until you reach th___

2 **When you call EMS, be ready to provide the following infor**

Your name _____

Type of emergency _____

Location of emergency _____
  street address

  _____
  apartment number

  _____
  nearby landmarks

  _____
  major intersections

Telephone number you're calling from _____

How many are injured? _____

DON'T HANG UP UNTIL THE DISPATCHER TELL

VOCABULARY: Writing with Vocabulary Words

Use five or more of the following words or phrases to write a paragraph that tells how you can handle home emergencies.

emergency
ambulance
operator
unconscious
smoke detector
fire extinguisher

_____

_____

_____

_____

_____

COMPREHENSION: Circle the Answer

Draw a circle around the correct answer.

1. Which supplies do you need to keep in your home for an emergency? (Circle all that are correct.)

    flashlight   ice cream   electric can opener   blankets

    candles   matches   battery radio   first-aid kit

2. How often do you need to check the batteries in a smoke detector?

    every day   once a month   once a year

3. What will put out an oil fire?

    water   more oil   baking soda

4. What do you need to do if you smell gas?

    Call the gas company from your neighbor's phone.

    Open all windows.

    Turn on the oven.

Thinking and Writing

Imagine hearing a weather report that says your area will be hit by a hurricane tomorrow. Explain in your journal how you would prepare.

CHAPTER 8

PREVENTING ACCIDENTS AT HOME

THINK ABOUT AS YOU READ

- Why do drivers need to avoid using alcohol and certain kinds of medicine when driving?
- How can you prevent poisoning in your home?
- How can you prevent kitchen and bathroom accidents?

Bike riding is one of Lisa Green's favorite sports. She is a careful rider who always wears a helmet. Her bike has good brakes and enough air in both tires. Lisa wears light-colored clothes when she rides so that drivers can see her easily. To avoid accidents, Lisa obeys all traffic rules.

Each year many people are hurt and killed in accidents. By learning good safety habits, you can prevent many kinds of accidents.

Good safety habits prevent injuries. Wear a helmet when you ride a bike.

Be sure you have the correct amount of air in your tires.

Safety for Bike Riders and Drivers

You may ride a bike to travel to work or to school. You can also make bike riding a sport that you enjoy. To ride safely, ride a bike that is the right size for you. Both children and adults need helmets whenever they ride. Use hand signals when you make turns or stops. It is dangerous to wear headphones when riding a bike.

Safety is also important when driving a car. It is against the law to drink alcohol and drive a car. More than half of all car accidents are caused by drivers who have been drinking alcohol. Even a small amount of alcohol can make it easier for you to get into an accident.

It is dangerous to drive when taking any medicine that can cause **drowsiness.** Check with your doctor or pharmacist to learn if your prescription medicines can make you sleepy. Check the warning labels on all over-the-counter drugs. Sometimes the label will tell you not to drive because a certain medicine causes drowsiness.

Be sure your car has been checked for safety. Your car needs good brakes and tires. If you are buying a car, try to buy one that has air bags. All passengers need to wear seat belts at all times.

Drowsiness means feeling sleepy.

Small children need to ride in special safety seats in cars. A seat belt alone cannot protect a small child. Small babies need a different kind of seat than a child who can sit and walk. Use the right kind of seats for the children who ride in your car. To be safe, these seats need to be used correctly. So follow the directions that come with car seats for children.

Preventing Falls and Poisoning

Many people are hurt each year because they fall in their own homes. To prevent falls, wear shoes and not just socks when walking around your home. It is easy to slip on floors that have too much wax. So avoid using too much wax. Wipe all spills from the floor as soon as they happen. Do not leave objects on the floor or steps that people can trip on. Put rubber mats under small loose rugs so they do not move when you walk on them.

Many of the cleaning products, medicines, and beauty products in your home are poisonous. Check the warning labels on your **detergent,** paints, nail polish remover, and hair spray. All of these products are poisonous, too. Products like paint and hair spray are poisonous if swallowed. Some products can harm you if you breathe in their **fumes.**

Detergent is soap that can be used for cleaning clothes, dishes, floors, and other parts of a home.

Fumes are the gases given off by products like paint and nail polish.

Make sure children are buckled up in car seats.

80

Follow these rules to prevent poisoning.

1. Store all medicines, make-up, cleaning products, and beauty products on a high shelf that children cannot reach. If possible, keep these supplies in a locked closet.

2. Never put poisonous products like detergent in food containers. Keep poisonous products in the containers they came in. Leave the warning labels on the containers.

3. Teach children not to eat house plants. Many house plants are poisonous.

4. Keep the windows open when using paints, paint thinners, and other products that give off fumes.

Poisons can kill people fast. Get help quickly if you believe a person swallowed a poison. Call your Poison Control Center. Keep the phone number of your Poison Control Center by your phone near the EMS number. Tell the person at the center which poison was swallowed. The person at the center will tell you what to do. Sometimes the poison victim is unconscious. Then you may not know what kind of poison was swallowed. Call EMS for help at once. Call EMS if someone becomes sick from breathing poisonous fumes.

CAUTION:
Avoid contact with eyes, skin, and mucous membranes. Do not mix with acids or other household chemicals. In case of eye contact, flush thoroughly with water. If swallowed, give one or two glasses of water or milk. Call physician. Use only in well ventilated areas. Do not use on fabrics or surfaces which may be discolored or damaged. Rinse immediately upon contact with porcelain tu
KEEP OUT OF REACH OF CHILDREN.

CAUTION: If swallowed, give a glassful of water or milk. Call a physician. In case of eye contact, flush with water. KEEP OUT OF REACH OF CHILDREN.

WARNING:
Precautionary Statements
Hazards to humans and domestic animals.
Causes substantial but temporary eye injury. Do not get in eyes or on clothing. Harmful if swallowed. May irritate skin. For prolonged use, wear gloves.
Practical treatment. If in eyes, remove contact lenses and rinse with plenty of water for 15 minutes. If swallowed, drink a glassful of water. Call physician in either case. If in contact with skin, immediately remove contaminated clothing and wash skin thoroughly with water.

Read and follow the warning labels on household products.

81

Preventing Kitchen and Bathroom Accidents

Most home accidents happen in the kitchen and bathroom. These safety rules can help you avoid accidents.

1. If you have young children in your home, put child-proof locks on all kitchen and bathroom cabinets.

2. Do not leave young children alone in the kitchen or bathroom.

3. Never hang kitchen towels above the stove to dry.

4. In the bathroom use plastic cups and bottles that cannot break.

5. Dry your hands before using hair dryers and other electric appliances.

6. Do not stand in a puddle of water when using an electric appliance. You can get an electric shock.

7. Use a rubber bath mat in your tub and shower to prevent falls.

8. Never use an electric heater in your bathroom or near your kitchen sink. You may get an electric shock.

To child-proof your home, put child-proof locks on cabinets.

Preventing Other Home Accidents

Many home fires are caused by burning cigarettes. Dangerous fires can start when people smoke cigarettes in bed. Never allow anyone in your home to smoke in bed.

Your home needs a smoke detector that works. Check the batteries once a month. Your smoke detector will warn you if a fire is starting.

Guns are dangerous weapons to have in a home. If you own a gun, always keep it in a locked closet. Keep bullets in a separate locked closet.

Electricity can be dangerous if it is not used carefully. Cover electric outlets with safety covers to prevent children from playing with them. Sometimes the **fuse** in your home will blow if you use too many appliances at once. Always replace a blown fuse with another fuse that is the same size.

The chart on this page shows other ways to use electricity safely.

Take a walk through your home and see where accidents can happen. Make those parts of your home safer. Learning how to prevent accidents will help you have good health and enjoy life.

A **fuse** is a safety wire that melts and shuts off the electricity when too much electricity is used at one time.

Use the right size light bulbs for your lamps.

Do not put too many plugs in one outlet.

Keep electric appliances away from children.

Using Electricity Safely

Repair damaged electrical cords.

Use the right kind of extension cord for your appliance.

Unplug appliances that are not in use.

HOME SAFETY

Problem	How to Be Safe
Being safe at home	1. Never open the door for a person without first checking to find out who wants to come in. 2. Never allow strangers to come into your home. 3. Call 9-1-1 or the operator if there is an emergency. 4. Use good locks on your front and back doors. 5. Lock all doors and windows when you leave your home. 6. Keep your EMS number and your Poison Control Center number near your phone.
Poisons	1. Buy medicines and cleansers in childproof containers. 2. Check expiration dates on all medicines. Flush old medicine down the toilet. Check with your pharmacist if you have questions. 3. Keep all poisons, chemicals, and medicines in places children cannot reach. 4. Keep chemicals, cleansers, and medicines in their containers. 5. Call the Poison Control Center or EMS before you try to help someone who has swallowed a poison.
Food poisoning	1. Never eat food from rusted, leaking, or swollen cans. 2. Check expiration dates on food. Do not eat food that is older than the expiration date. 3. Wash tops of cans before opening them. 4. Do not eat raw meat, chicken, fish, or eggs.
Kitchen accidents	1. Do not leave small children alone in the kitchen. 2. Never allow children to play with plastic bags. 3. Do not wear long, loose sleeves when cooking. They can catch on fire. 4. Keep rags, paper, and towels away from the stove. 5. Keep a fire extinguisher in the kitchen to put out fires. Know how to use it to put out fires.
Accidents in the bathroom	1. Use plastic cups and bottles. 2. Wipe all spills from the floor. 3. Never leave small children alone in the bathroom. Never leave small children alone in the bathtub. 4. Do not leave medicine in a medicine chest that small children can reach or open. 5. Never use electrical appliances in or near water.
Storage areas	1. Do not keep old clothes, newspapers, and furniture that people no longer use. 2. Keep storage areas locked so children cannot go into them. 3. Keep flammable liquids in their containers. Keep flammable liquids away from heat or fire.

Reading Warning Labels

All over-the-counter drugs come with warnings on their labels. The warning label below is for the over-the-counter drug Benadryl. People with colds and allergies take this drug to feel better. Notice the warnings on the label.

WARNINGS: Do not take this product if you have asthma, glaucoma, emphysema, chronic pulmonary disease, shortness of breath, difficulty in breathing or difficulty in urination due to enlargement of the prostate gland unless directed by a physician. May cause excitability especially in children. May cause marked drowsiness; alcohol, sedatives, and tranquilizers may increase the drowsiness effect. Avoid driving a motor vehicle or operating machinery or drinking alcoholic beverages. Do not take this product if you are taking sedatives or tranquilizers without first consulting your doctor. Do not use any other products containing diphenhydramine while using this product. As with any drug, if you are pregnant or nursing a baby, seek the advice of a health professional before using this product. **KEEP THIS AND ALL DRUGS OUT OF THE REACH OF CHILDREN.** In case of accidental overdose, seek professional assistance or contact a Poison Control Center immediately.

■ ■ ■

Answer these questions about the warning label on Benadryl.

1. Who should not take Benadryl?

   _____

   _____

2. What side effects can the drug cause?

   _____

   _____

3. What do you need to avoid doing when taking Benadryl?

   _____

   _____

4. What do you need to do if you take an overdose?

   _____

   _____

WORKSHOP PRACTICE: Read a Warning Label

The Necessary Skills Workshop showed you how to read warning labels on medicines. It is also important for you to read the warning labels on other products in your home. Read the warning label from a can of paint. Then answer the questions.

CAUTION: MAY CAUSE EYE AND SKIN IRRITATION ON CONTACT. INHALATION OF SPRAY MIST MAY CAUSE RESPIRATORY TRACT IRRITATION. MAY BE HARMFUL IF SWALLOWED.

FIRST AID: In case of skin contact, wash off quickly with soap and water. For eye contact, flush immediately with large amounts of water, especially under lids. Always paint with adequate ventilation. If inhalation causes irritation or other discomfort, move to fresh air. If discomfort or irritation persists, seek medical attention.

IMPORTANT! Spray mist contains particles that may cause irritation of respiratory tract if inhaled. If this paint is spray applied, the use of a respirator is recommended. Obtain professional advice for proper selection, fit, and use of respirator. If sanding of any paint is done, wear a dust mask.

For emergency information call (800) 545-2643.
For additional information, refer to the Material Safety Data Sheet for this product.

KEEP OUT OF REACH OF CHILDREN.

---

1. How can paint be harmful? _____

_____

2. What should you do if paint gets in your eyes? _____

_____

3. If you have trouble breathing, what do you need to do?

_____

_____

VOCABULARY: Find the Meaning

On the line write the word or phrase that best completes each sentence.

1. Medicine that makes you sleepy causes _____ .

drowsiness   happiness   high blood pressure

2. A person who has passed out and cannot feel things or move is

_____ .

awake unconscious dreaming

3. Soaps that are used for cleaning dishes, clothes, floors, and other parts

of the home are _____ .

deodorants detergents wax

4. The gases given off by products like paint and nail polish remover are

_____ .

fuses nutrients fumes

5. A _____ is a safety wire that melts and shuts off the
power when too much electricity is used at one time.

fuse appliance fume

COMPREHENSION: True or False

Write True next to each sentence that is true. Write False next to each sentence that
is false. There are two false sentences.

_____ 1. It is against the law to drink alcohol and drive a car.

_____ 2. Passengers always need to wear seat belts in cars.

_____ 3. It is safe to wear headphones when riding a bike.

_____ 4. Call EMS if you do not know what kind of poison
a person swallowed.

_____ 5. Close your windows when using paint and paint thinners.

On the lines that follow, rewrite the two false sentences to make them true.

_____

_____

**Thinking and
Writing**

What areas of your home could be made safer? What could
you change to improve the safety in your home? Explain in
your journal how you can make your home safer.

CROSSWORD PUZZLE: Safety First

Use the clues below to complete the crossword puzzle on page 89.
Choose from the words listed on page 89.
For an extra challenge, cover up the words.

Across

3. A _____ is a doctor who treats children.

5. A _____ is a safety wire that melts and shuts off the electricity when too much electricity is used at one time.

6. A germ that causes a disease and cannot be killed by antibiotics is a _____ .

8. The _____ is the part of your body that is below your chest and above your hips.

9. A _____ pad is free from germs and dirt.

10. A government health insurance program to provide health care for people with low incomes is _____ .

Down

1. Germs that cause diseases and that can be killed by antibiotics are _____ .

2. A _____ is a person who is sick or hurt.

3. A _____ is a written order from a doctor for a certain type of medicine.

4. _____ means feeling sleepy.

5. The emergency care given to a hurt or sick person until that person can see a doctor is _____ .

7. An _____ is medicine that can kill certain bacteria that cause illness.

abdomen

antibiotic

bacteria

drowsiness

first aid

fuse

Medicaid

pediatrician

prescription

sterile

victim

virus

CHAPTER 9

PREVENTING CRIME AT HOME

THINK ABOUT AS YOU READ

- How can you protect yourself from crime?
- How can you keep burglars out of your home?
- What can you do to prevent crime at home?

When a home is **burglarized,** someone has broken into it to steal.

A **crime** is an act, like murder, that is against the law.

Sandra Marks heard that her neighbor's apartment was **burglarized.** She was afraid that her apartment would be burglarized, too. She decided to do everything possible to prevent burglary of her home. In this chapter you will learn how you can prevent **crime** in your home.

Crimes at Home

You want your home to be a safe place to live. But crimes can take place in your home.

Protect your home from burglary.

Report all crimes to the police at once.

Burglary is the most common type of crime. **Sexual assault** and **homicide** are other crimes that can happen in the home. Often the attacker is someone the victim knows. Arguments among friends and family can end in homicide. Often drugs and alcohol cause people to lose control in arguments at home.

The attacker may be a stranger. Most **burglars** want to enter a home when no one is there. If a victim surprises a burglar, a burglary may end in homicide.

Report all crimes to the police at once. Do not touch anything before the police get to the place of the crime. The police will ask you questions. If you were sexually assaulted, the police will have a doctor check your body for proof. So do not bathe or shower until you have seen a doctor. This proof will be used in court against the attacker. If your home is burglarized, you will be asked for a list of things that were taken by the burglar. The police will use the information to try to find the stolen goods.

You can help protect yourself and your home from crimes. Never allow strangers into your home. Give a key to your home only to people that you really trust.

Sexual assault happens when an attacker uses force to perform sexual acts on another person.

Homicide is the killing of one person by another person.

A **burglar** is a person who enters the homes and businesses of others in order to steal.

Keeping Burglars Out of Your Home

Burglars look for homes that are easy to enter and easy to leave. They do not want neighbors to see them. They look for places where no one is at home.

To protect your home, make it hard for a burglar to enter. Here are some ways you can try to protect your home from crime.

1. Make your home look as if you are there. Keep your kitchen and living room lights on a timer. The timer can turn the lights on each night when you are away from home. It can turn lights off at about midnight. You can also put a radio on a timer.

2. Never leave the key to your home outside near the door. Burglars know to look for a key under a doormat or large plant.

3. Have outdoor lights on around your home at night to make it easier for a burglar to be seen.

4. Close your drapes, blinds, or shades at night. Open them during the day.

5. Leave a key to your home with a neighbor that you trust. When you are away, the neighbor can open and close your drapes, blinds, or shades. The neighbor can let the police in if there is a problem.

An **engraving pen** is a tool that can make marks on plastic and metal. The marks cannot be removed easily.

6. Use an **engraving pen** to write your name on your TV, camera, stereo, and other expensive items. Also write your driver's license number, Social Security number, or other identification number on each item. It is much harder for a burglar to sell stolen goods that are marked with such identification. Also have a list of the make, model, and serial number of your property.

7. Lock all doors and windows when you leave. Check that they are locked before going to sleep at night.

8. Be careful when you go out of town. You want your home to look as if people are there. Ask a neighbor to collect your mail each day. Ask your neighbor to pick up newspapers and other papers left at your front door. If you plan to be out of town for a couple of weeks, have your newspaper delivery stopped while you are away.

9. Do not keep large amounts of money in your home.

10. Never put your address on your keys. If you lose your keys, the person who finds them can enter your home.

11. Never enter your home if you think a burglar or attacker may be inside. Go to the nearest phone and call the police.

Making Your Home Safer

Burglars enter homes through doors and windows. Try to make your doors and windows hard for a burglar to open.

Don't let burglars know that you are gone. Have a neighbor pick up your newspapers.

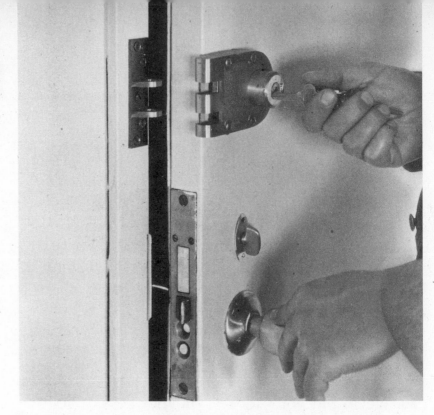

A **peephole** is a small hole in a door. It allows you to see outside without opening the door.

A **deadbolt** is a type of lock that offers good protection against burglars.

A **pickproof lock** is a lock that needs to be opened with a key. It cannot be opened by a burglar.

You need a strong front door. If you live in a private house, you need a strong back door, too. Burglars often enter through back doors because fewer people will see them. Some front doors have large glass in them. Avoid buying these doors. Burglars can break the glass and unlock the door to enter the house. Have a **peephole** in your front door. Always look through the peephole before opening the door. Decide if you want to allow the person to enter your home.

Every outside door of your home needs good locks. You want locks that will be hard for a burglar to open. Get **deadbolt** locks that are **pickproof.** Ask your landlord to give you new locks when you move into your home.

You might want to have two locks on your front and back doors. Two locks are much more work to open than one lock. When burglars see doors with two locks, they often leave without even trying to break in.

Many burglars break into homes through the windows. Make sure your windows are very hard to open from outside. Have locks on all windows.

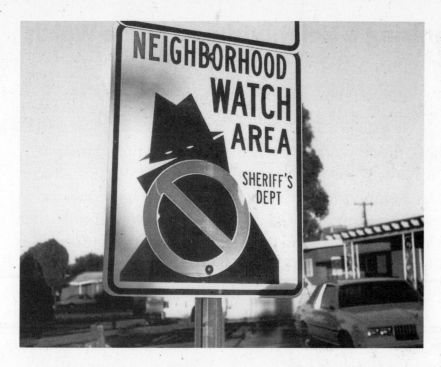

Find out how to set up a Neighborhood Crime Watch in your area.

A fire escape window needs a lock that can be opened without a key. You will need to be able to escape quickly through that window if there is a fire in your home.

Another way to prevent crime is with a **burglar alarm.** The alarm rings when a burglar tries to enter the home. You can put a sticker on your front door that says your home has an alarm system. Many burglars avoid homes with alarms.

A dog can also frighten burglars away. Most dogs bark when strangers come near. Some burglars are afraid they will be noticed when a dog starts barking. They are afraid the dog will attack them if they enter the home. So they try to avoid homes that have dogs. If you do not have a dog, you can put out a large dog dish or have a tape recording of a large dog barking.

You have the right to be safe from crime, especially in your own home. Choose good locks for your doors and windows. Think about putting a burglar alarm in your home. Look through your peephole before opening your door. Never let strangers into your home. By protecting yourself from crime, you will enjoy living in your own home.

A **burglar alarm** is an appliance that makes a loud ringing noise if someone tries to break into a home.

Organizing a Neighborhood Crime Watch

In many cities neighbors are joining together to prevent crime. They organize a Neighborhood Crime Watch.

A Neighborhood Crime Watch is a way to reduce crimes at home. It is a way for people to join with the police to reduce crimes. A Neighborhood Crime Watch works in two ways. First, it allows people to find out when they should call police. You need to call the police after a crime has taken place. But you can also call the police when you see something strange going on that you think may lead to a crime.

Second, a Neighborhood Crime Watch allows people to find out how to make their homes safer. Police give information to people about how to protect themselves from crime. As new information comes out, police tell the people about it.

The Neighborhood Crime Watch is a group effort. All the people living in the area can take part in it. It helps everybody stay safe from crime.

CRIME IN OUR NEIGHBORHOOD

Let's Do Something About It!

NEIGHBORHOOD WATCH

Here is how you can start a Neighborhood Crime Watch on your block.

1. Call the crime prevention unit of your police department. Get information from the police about the Neighborhood Crime Watch program.

2. Speak to the people on your block. Tell them what a Neighborhood Crime Watch means. Explain that it can lower crime in the neighborhood. Everyone will feel safer and friendlier.

3. Organize a block meeting with people on the block. At the block meeting, elect a leader. The leader will be called the block captain. The block captain will be the contact with the police. The police will give information about crime prevention to the block captain. The block captain will then give the information to the people in the group.

4. Members of the Neighborhood Crime Watch Group attend a few special meetings with the police. The police teach members how to make their homes safer. Members learn how to prevent attacks.

5. Members learn to look out and care for each other. They call the police when they think there may be a burglar or an attacker in the neighborhood.

6. Group members can buy a Crime Watch sign from the police. They put the sign in their neighborhood. It warns burglars and attackers that the neighbors are watching out for them. The groups can buy these signs when they have enough members.

■ ■ ■

Answer these questions about having a Neighborhood Crime Watch Group.

1. How can a Neighborhood Crime Watch help your neighborhood?

_____

_____

2. What does the block captain do?

_____

_____

3. What do members learn at their meetings with the police?

_____

_____

WORKSHOP PRACTICE: Start a Crime Watch Group

A Neighborhood Crime Watch can make your home and your neighborhood safer. Explain six things you and your neighbors can do to start a Crime Watch Group. Look back at pages 96–97.

1. _____

_____

_____

2. _____

_____

_____

3. _____

_____

_____

4. _____

_____

_____

5. _____

_____

_____

6. _____

_____

_____

VOCABULARY: Finish the Sentence

Choose one of the following words or phrases to complete each sentence.
Write the word or phrase on the correct line.

crimes
sexual assault
homicide
deadbolt lock

1. _____ are actions like murder and burglary that are against the law.

2. A _____ is the killing of one person by another.

3. Using force to perform sexual acts on another person is called _____ .

4. A type of lock that offers good protection from burglars is a _____ .

COMPREHENSION: Finish the Paragraph

Use the following words or phrases to finish the paragraph. Write the words you choose on the correct lines.

police
key
strangers
peephole
pickproof
windows

To protect yourself and your home, you need to try to keep _____ out of your home. Never open your door without looking through the _____ . Never leave your _____ under a doormat. When leaving your home, always lock all doors and _____ . Have locks for your doors that are _____ . Report all crimes to the _____ at once.

Thinking and Writing

Why does your home always need to look as if you are there? What can you do to make sure your home looks as if you are always there? Explain your answers in your journal.

CHAPTER 10

GOVERNMENT SERVICES AVAILABLE TO HELP YOU

THINK ABOUT AS YOU READ

- What services do state and local governments provide?
- What government programs help people with low incomes?
- What are some services provided by the federal government?

Karen Parker began using government services as soon as she left for work in the morning. First, she walked her son to public school. Then she rode on a city bus to her job. Before starting her job, Karen stopped at a post office to buy stamps. After work, Karen visited her sick mother. Her mother was being cared for in a city hospital.

The government is part of your life every day. You depend on the government for many kinds of services.

You use government services every day.

Local and State Government Services

You use the services of your state and local
governments every day. These governments collect
garbage. They provide clean drinking water. They
provide the money for public schools and libraries.

Your local government keeps many records. It
keeps a record of every birth, death, marriage, and
divorce. Very soon after birth, every child is given a
birth certificate. Your local government prepares a
death certificate for each person who dies.

Your state has programs to help you if your
income is low. Low-income families with children
under age 18 can receive money from the
government twice a month. This program is called
Aid to Families with Dependent Children, or
AFDC. Families use this money to pay for food,
clothing, housing, and medicine. People with low
incomes can also receive food stamps to help them
buy food. Every state also helps people with low
incomes pay for medical care. This program is called
Medicaid. It helps pay for doctor and hospital bills.

A **birth certificate**
is a paper from your
local government that
has information about
your name, birth, and
parents.

**Aid to Families with
Dependent Children
(AFDC)** is a program
that provides money
to low-income families
with children. The
federal and state
governments share the
cost of this program.

Every state provides a
Medicaid program to
help people with low
incomes pay for medical
care. This program is
paid for by the states
and the federal
government.

A **state employment agency** can help you find a job. You do not pay the agency for this service.

If you lose your job, your state's **unemployment insurance** program may pay part of your salary while you look for work.

Your state's **workers' compensation** program may pay part of your salary and medical bills if you get hurt or sick while working.

The federal government has passed laws that say states have to provide money, food stamps, and Medicaid to low-income families. Each state receives some money from the federal government for these programs. Then each state decides how to run these programs to meet the needs of the people in that state.

Your state also has programs to help workers. If you need a job, a **state employment agency** in your area may help you find one. These agencies receive money from the federal government.

Every state has a program called **unemployment insurance.** This program may pay part of your salary if you lose your job. If you lose your job, visit your state's unemployment office to find out if you can receive this kind of insurance.

Every state also has a program called **workers' compensation.** This program helps people who get hurt while working. You may be able to receive money from this program if you are hurt at your job.

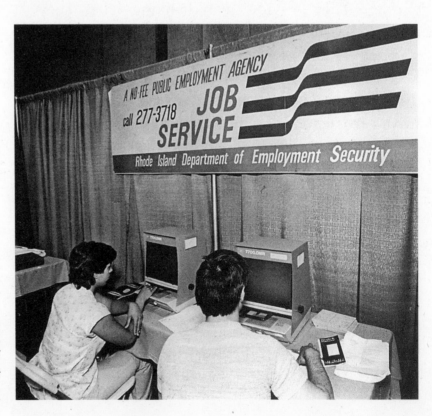

Your state government provides a state employment agency to help you find a job.

Federal Government Services

Every year many people move to the United States from other countries. These people need permission papers to live and work in the United States. This type of paper is called a green card. You can get a green card from a federal agency called **Immigration and Naturalization Services,** or **INS.** This agency has many offices throughout the country.

Immigration and Naturalization Services also helps people from other countries become **citizens** of the United States. An adult who is 18 years or older and has lived in this country for five years can try to become a citizen. To become a citizen, you have to complete INS forms and meet with an INS officer. After you become a citizen, you will have the same rights as a person who was born in this nation. The only difference is that you cannot become President or Vice President of the United States.

Immigration and Naturalization Services (INS) is a federal agency that helps people from other nations get legal papers to live in the United States. It also helps people become American citizens.

Citizens are members of a nation and have the rights of that nation.

EIGHT FEDERAL AGENCIES AND THEIR SERVICES

Agency	Services
Immigration and Naturalization Services	Helps people from other nations get green cards and become citizens
Food Safety and Inspection Service	Checks and grades meat, chicken, turkey, and dairy products
Social Security Administration	Provides Social Security income and medical insurance to older people and people with disabilities
Federal Bureau of Investigation (FBI)	Finds evidence about crimes for the federal government
Internal Revenue Service	Collects federal income taxes
Food and Drug Administration	Checks food and medicine for safety
Equal Employment Opportunity Commission	Carries out laws to end job discrimination
Food and Nutrition Service	Provides food stamps and school breakfast and lunch programs

You use other services of the federal government. Federal agencies make all of the money used in this country. The federal government makes all stamps. It runs all post offices. The federal government also gives money to the states for job training programs. Through one of these programs, you may get a better job.

Most people who earn income have to pay taxes to the Internal Revenue Service, or IRS. This federal agency also has a program that helps people who work and have low incomes. This program is called Earned Income Tax Credit. If you are a worker with a low income, this program may help you pay less federal income tax. Then you can keep more of the money you earn. You may even receive money from the IRS. To learn more about this program, call an IRS office near your home.

Federal agencies help you in other ways. An agency called the **Food and Drug Administration,** or **FDA,** checks all new medicines. It makes sure that medicines really do what their companies say they will do. This agency does not allow unsafe medicines to be sold.

The **Food and Drug Administration (FDA)** is a federal agency that checks the safety of foods, medicines, and make-up.

Another federal agency checks your food. The agency makes sure that meat, fish, and eggs are healthy and safe. Another agency gives money to states for food stamps. This agency also gives money to states for school breakfast and lunch programs.

Using Government Services

There are many government services that can help you. Many of these services are run by state and local governments. You can get information from your state and local governments about the services they provide. In many states you can get this information by calling the **department of social services.**

The **Department of Housing and Urban Development,** or **HUD,** is a federal agency that offers low-cost housing. HUD gives money to each state to help people with low incomes find housing. Some of this money is used to help people pay rent. Other money is used to pay for apartments in public housing. These apartments are in buildings that belong to the government. Some states use HUD money to give loans to people with low incomes. Then they can buy their own homes.

The government also provides you with a small income when you stop working after the age of 62. This income is called Social Security. If you die before age 62, the government may pay money to your children and your wife or husband. The amount of income depends on how many years you worked. It also depends on how much money you paid into the plan.

Federal, state, and local governments provide hundreds of services. Postage stamps, money, schools, and safe medicines are just some of the services you use. Government is part of your life every day.

The **department of social services** is an agency that helps people with disabilities, people with low incomes, and older adults get many kinds of services. In some states it may be called the department of human services.

The **Department of Housing and Urban Development (HUD)** is part of the federal government. It helps people with low incomes find housing that they can afford.

Getting a Copy of Your Birth Certificate

A birth certificate is a record of your birth. You may be asked to show your birth certificate to prove your age or date of birth. You have to have a birth certificate to get a Social Security card or a passport.

If you have lost your birth certificate, you can get a copy of it from your local government. Some local governments keep birth certificates and other records in a place called the vital records office. Find out where your local government keeps birth certificates and other records. Find out how much your government charges for a copy of your birth certificate.

You can get a copy of your birth certificate by writing a letter to the vital records office of the county where you were born. Include a check for the correct amount of money with your letter. Your letter needs to have the following information.

1. Your full name at birth.

2. Your date of birth.

3. The place of your birth. Include the town or county.

4. Your present home address.

5. Your father's full name.

6. Your mother's maiden name. (This is your mother's last name when she was born.)

7. The reason that you need a copy of the birth certificate.

Karen Parker needed a copy of her birth certificate. She wrote the letter on page 107 to get an official copy.

■■■

Use Karen's letter to answer the following questions.

1. Why does Karen need a copy of her birth certificate? _____

2. Where was Karen born? _____

3. What maiden name did Karen's mother have? _____

4. What is the cost of a birth certificate in Little Rock? _____

170 West 11th Street
Little Rock, AR 72202
March 18, 1994

Vital Records Office
Department of Health
4815 W. Markham Street
Slot 44
Little Rock, AR 72205

To Whom It May Concern:

Please send me an official copy of my birth certificate. I need it to get a passport. Here is the information you need.

My full name at birth: Karen Sue Jackson
My date of birth: October 17, 1961
My place of birth: Pulaski County
My father's name: David Sam Jackson
My mother's maiden name: Linda Butler
My home address: 170 West 11th Street, Little Rock, AR 72202

There is a $5 check in this envelope to pay for the cost of the birth certificate. Please send it to me as soon as possible.

Thank you.

Sincerely,

Karen Parker

Karen Parker

WORKSHOP PRACTICE: Write a Letter for a Birth Certificate

On the lines below, write the information you would need to get a copy of your birth certificate. Then use the information to write a letter asking for a birth certificate. Write your letter on another sheet of paper.

1. County where you were born _____

2. Address of vital records office _____

   _____

   _____

3. Full name at birth _____

4. Date of birth _____

5. Place of birth _____

6. Father's full name _____

7. Mother's maiden name _____

8. Present address _____

COMPREHENSION: True or False

Write True next to each sentence that is true. Write False next to each sentence that is false. There are two false sentences.

_____ 1. The program called Aid to Families with Dependent Children gives money to low-income families with children.

_____ 2. The federal government keeps records of births, deaths, marriages, and divorces.

_____ 3. The INS is a federal agency that helps people from other nations get green cards and become citizens.

_____ 4. Earned Income Tax Credit is a program that helps people with low incomes pay less taxes.

_____ 5. Each state has an agency to make sure new medicines are safe.

On the lines that follow, rewrite the two false sentences to make them true.

_____

_____

_____

_____

VOCABULARY: Finish the Sentence

Choose one of the following words or phrases to complete each sentence. Write the word or phrase on the correct line.

citizens
Food and Drug Administration
Department of Housing and Urban Development
Medicaid
state employment agency
workers' compensation

1. Your state's _____ program helps people with low incomes pay for medical care.

2. Your _____ helps people find jobs and does not charge for its services.

3. Members of a nation are called _____ .

4. A person who gets sick or hurt from working at a job may get money called

   _____ .

5. The _____ helps low-income people find housing that they can afford.

6. The _____ checks all new medicines.

Thinking and Writing

Sometimes federal, state, and local governments try to save money by providing fewer services. Think about the agencies and services discussed in Chapter 10. Look at the chart on page 104 again. What services do you think the government could stop providing? Which ones are really necessary? In your journal explain how governments could save money.

CHAPTER 11

VOTING IN ELECTIONS

THINK ABOUT AS YOU READ

- Who has the right to vote in American elections?
- Why do some people have to register to vote more than once?
- How can you get the information you need to decide how to vote?

Van Deng Cong moved to the United States from Vietnam. In Vietnam he did not enjoy freedom of speech. It was dangerous to speak against the government. He could be sent to jail without a fair trial. Van Deng left his country and moved to the United States. After Van Deng became a citizen, he was proud to vote in American **elections.**

Americans choose their leaders by voting in elections. Each time you vote, you have a voice in your government.

An **election** is an event in which people choose leaders by voting.

Americans vote in elections to choose government leaders.

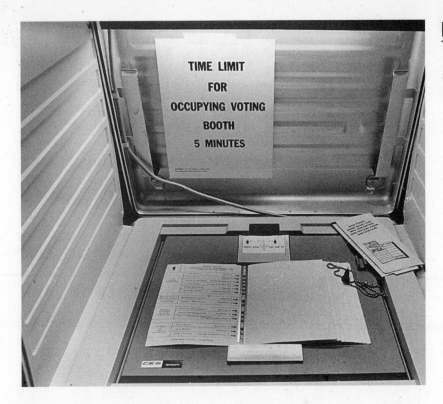

Different voting areas may use different types of voting machines.

Your Right to Vote

The Constitution gives Americans the right to vote. There are four rules about who can vote.

1. You have to be 18 or older.

2. You have to be an American citizen. If you were not born in the United States, you can become a citizen through Immigration and Naturalization Services, or INS.

3. You have to live in your state for a certain amount of time. Each state has its own laws about the amount of time you have to live there before you can vote.

4. You have to register to vote.

The Constitution protects your right to vote. You cannot lose your right to vote because of your race, sex, or religion. You cannot lose it because you speak against the government. But people who are in prison lose their right to vote.

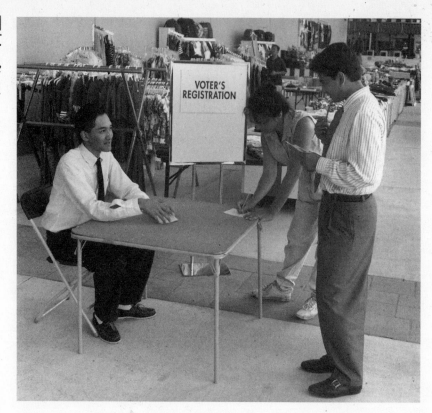

You need to register before you can vote in an election.

Your right to vote allows you to vote in federal, state, and local elections. You can vote to help choose the President of the United States. You can also vote for many other leaders and lawmakers.

In an election every vote counts. The **candidate** who gets the most votes becomes the winner. Sometimes a candidate wins by only a few votes. Your vote can help a candidate win or lose.

A **candidate** is a person who is trying to get elected to a job in government.

Register to Vote

In 49 states people have to register in order to vote. North Dakota is the only state where you do not have to register before you can vote.

Every state has its own rules about how to register. Most states allow you to register in person or by mail. Some states allow you to register at banks, public schools, and libraries. You have to complete a voter registration form. You do not pay a fee when you register. The Necessary Skills Workshop in this chapter shows you how to complete a voter registration form.

Find out the rules for voter registration in your state. Learn how many days before an election you have to register to vote. In some states you can get information by calling a voter registration office. In other states you can get information by calling the Board of Elections. You can also get information by calling the nearest office of the League of Women Voters.

In some states when you register to vote, you can also join a **political party.** There may be a place on your registration form to register to be a member of a political party. You do not have to pay to join a political party. The **Democratic** and **Republican** parties are the two largest political parties in our nation. Members of political parties work together to reach goals. They work together to help their candidates win elections. You may want to do **volunteer work** to help your political party. You do not have to join a political party when you register to vote.

Sometimes you have to register to vote more than once. If you do not vote for a few years, you will have to register again. Complete a new voter registration form if you want to change your political party. If you move to a new address or change your name, you need to register again.

A **political party** is a large group of people who have similar beliefs about government. This group will try to get members of their party elected.

The **Democratic Party** is one of the two largest American political parties.

The **Republican Party** is the other large political party.

Volunteer work is work that people are not paid to do. The work is done to help an organization.

Candidates try hard to build support.

Becoming a Smart Voter

To be a smart voter, you need information about the different candidates in an election. Learn what each candidate hopes to do after winning the election. Learn about the work the candidates have done before the election **campaign.** Use this information to decide how to vote.

You can get information about candidates by listening to news reports. Listen to the speeches the candidates make on TV and radio to learn their ideas. Newspaper and magazine articles can help you learn about the candidates.

As you find information, learn the difference between facts and **opinions** about the candidates. Facts are true information. Opinions are statements that tell you what some people think about the candidate. For example, an opinion might be that one candidate is smarter than the other. You can disagree with the opinions other people may have about a candidate. Use the facts about the candidates to form your own opinions. In your opinion one candidate may be a better choice than the other. Your opinions will help you decide how to vote.

A smart voter also pays attention to campaign ads. There are ads on radio and TV and in newspapers. Sometimes ads contain information that is not completely true. By learning the facts about a candidate, you will know when the ads are correct.

In most states only members of a political party can vote in **primary elections.** In the primary election, you vote for a person to be the candidate of your political party. Your party's winning candidate will run against the candidate from the other party in the main election. In most states to vote in a primary, you have to be registered as a Democrat or as a Republican. Learn as much as you can about each candidate before voting in a primary election.

A **campaign** is all the ways a candidate seeks support to win an election.

An **opinion** is a belief that tells how you think or feel about a person or event. The sentence "George Washington was our best president" is an opinion.

In a **primary election,** members of a political party elect their candidates for the main election.

Before an election, you may receive voting information in the mail. This information will tell you when and where to vote. You can also get this information by calling the Board of Elections. The League of Women Voters also provides this information. Your place to vote is called a **polling place.** You can find copies of the **ballot** in local newspapers. Study the ballot. Decide how you want to vote before going to your polling place on Election Day.

At every polling place, Americans vote with secret ballots. No one will know who you vote for. You have the right to vote for the candidate that you think is best.

Smart voters do not vote for candidates because of their race, sex, religion, or good looks. They do not vote for a candidate because their friends tell them to. They choose the candidates that they think will do the best job.

Every American has one vote on Election Day. When you vote, you have the same power as every other citizen in the nation. Use your vote to choose good leaders for America.

A **polling place** is the place where you vote. You are allowed to vote at only one polling place.

A **ballot** is a form used for voting. This form lists all the candidates.

How to Vote in an Election

① Find out how to register to vote in your state.

② Register to vote in person or by mail.

③ Register for a political party if you wish.

④ Learn about the candidates from your political party.

⑤ Find out the polling place where you are supposed to vote.

⑥ Vote in a primary election to choose the party's candidate.

⑦ Get information on candidates from both political parties.

⑧ Study the ballot before Election Day.

⑨ Go to your polling place and vote with a secret ballot.

Completing a Voter Registration Form

In every state except North Dakota, you have to register in order to vote. To register, you complete a voter registration form. You do not need to pay to register. It is against the law to charge a fee for registration. In most states you need to register at least 30 days before an election. After you complete the form, you can take it to the registration office. Most states allow you to mail the form to the registration office.

The voter registration form on page 117 is a sample of the form used by citizens in California. Most states ask for similar information on their registration forms. Read the form and the instructions for completing the **affidavit.** An affidavit is a legal form. **Perjury** is to swear to something that is not true. Perjury is against the law. Write only true information on a voter registration form. Note that you do not have to write your phone number on this voter registration form. It is marked "optional." If you do not want to join a political party, you can mark "Decline to State." This means you do not want to mark a certain political party.

After Van Deng Cong became an American citizen, he registered to vote. Then he moved to a new address. So he had to register again.

■ ■ ■

Use Van Deng's voter registration form to answer the following questions.

1. In what county does Van Deng live? _____

2. Which political party did Van Deng join? _____

3. Has Van Deng registered to vote before? yes _____ no _____

4. What was Van Deng's previous address? _____

_____

5. Was Van Deng a member of the Democratic Party when he lived on Prairie

Avenue? yes _____ no _____

6. Who helped Van Deng complete his form? _____

PRINT IN INK

STATE OF CALIFORNIA — AFFIDAVIT OF REGISTRATION

For U.S. Citizens Only

1 NAME (First Middle Last) — Optional ☒ Mr. ☐ Mrs. ☐ Miss ☐ Ms.

Van   Deng   Cong

2 RESIDENCE (Number – Street – Apartment No.)

260 West 6th Street   Apt. 3k

City: Los Angeles   County: Los Angeles County   ZIP Code: 90057

3 If no street address, describe location of residence: (cross streets, route, box, section, township, range, etc.)

4 MAILING ADDRESS (if different from residence)

City   State   ZIP Code

5 DATE OF BIRTH (Month – Day – Year)

09-06-59

6 BIRTHPLACE (U.S. State or Foreign Country)

Vietnam

7 POLITICAL PARTY (check one)
- ☐ American Independent Party
- ☒ Democratic Party
- ☐ Green Party
- ☐ Libertarian Party
- ☐ Peace and Freedom Party
- ☐ Republican Party
- ☐ Decline to State
- ☐ Other (Specify) _____

8 OCCUPATION

salesperson

9 Telephone (Optional) Area Code

(213) 555-6240

10 Not applicable in this County

11 HAVE YOU EVER BEEN REGISTERED TO VOTE? Yes ☒ No ☐

If yes, complete this section to the best of your knowledge concerning your **most recent** registration.

Name (as registered)

Van Deng Cong

Former Address

403 Prairie Avenue

City: Los Angeles   County: Los Angeles County   State: CA

Political Party

Democratic

READ THIS STATEMENT AND WARNING PRIOR TO SIGNING

I am a citizen of the United States and will be at least 18 years of age at the time of the next election. I am not imprisoned or on parole for the conviction of a felony. I certify under **penalty of perjury** under the laws of the State of California that the information on this affidavit is true and correct.

WARNING

Perjury is punishable by imprisonment in state prison for two, three or four years. §126 Penal Code

12 SIGNATURE — Sign on line in box below.

► Van Deng Cong

► Date 10-05-94   59 AD 609000

13 If someone helps fill out or keeps this form, see #13 instructions below.

(213) 555-3282

Tim Collins   10-05-94

INSTRUCTIONS FOR COMPLETING THE AFFIDAVIT

TYPE OR PRINT IN INK: Read instructions and information carefully. Only your "signature" should be written; all other information should be printed or typed.

WARNING—STATEMENT UNDER PENALTY OF PERJURY: Be sure you read the statement and warning above the signature line **prior** to signing your complete name. You must also date the affidavit. If you are 17 years of age, you may register to vote provided you will be 18 on or before the date of the next election.

1 Print your full name—first, middle, last.

2 Print your complete RESIDENCE ADDRESS (not P.O. box) including city and zip code. Enter street name to include North, South, East, West, if appropriate, and indicate whether it is a street, avenue, road, lane, drive, way, circle, etc.

3 If no street address, describe location of residence: (cross streets, route, box, section, township, range, etc.)

4 Print your complete mailing address if it is different from your residence address. Be sure to enter the route or box number, if any, and zip code.

5 Print your complete date of birth (month/day/year).

6 Print the name of the state in U.S.A. or foreign country where you were born.

7 IMPORTANT—POLITICAL PARTY: Place an "X" in the box preceding the qualified political party with which you wish to affiliate. You may print the name of an unqualified political party with which you wish to affiliate after "Other," or you may register as "Decline to State." IF YOU DO NOT AFFILIATE WITH A QUALIFIED POLITICAL PARTY, YOU WILL RECEIVE A NONPARTISAN BALLOT AND WILL NOT BE ALLOWED TO VOTE FOR PARTY CANDIDATES AT THE PRIMARY ELECTION.

8 Print your specific occupation (such as nurse, carpenter, homemaker, etc.).

9 OPTIONAL: Telephone number is optional. This number becomes public record if given. Please include Area Code.

10 Not applicable in this county (for official use only).

11 PRIOR REGISTRATION: If you have ever been registered to vote, complete this portion to the best of your knowledge concerning your most recent registration.

12 Sign your name as printed in Box 1. Date the affidavit below the signature box in the space provided.

13 Any person who helps someone fill out this form must include in Box 13 his/her signature and date.

WORKSHOP PRACTICE: Complete a Voter Registration Form

Complete the sample voter registration form on this page. Remember that this form is a sample. You cannot use it for your registration in any state. You have to use your state's voter registration form to register to vote.

PRINT IN INK   For U.S. Citizens Only

STATE OF CALIFORNIA — **AFFIDAVIT OF REGISTRATION**

1 NAME Optional (First   ☐Mr.   ☐Mrs.   ☐Miss   ☐Ms.
                    Middle   Last)

2 RESIDENCE (Number – Street – Apartment No.)

   City   County   ZIP Code

3 If no street address, describe location of residence: (cross streets, route, box, section, township, range, etc.)

4 MAILING ADDRESS (if different from residence)

   City   State   ZIP Code

5 DATE OF BIRTH (Month – Day – Year)   **8** OCCUPATION

6 BIRTHPLACE (U.S. State or Foreign Country)

7 POLITICAL PARTY (check one)   **9** Telephone (Optional)
   ☐ American Independent Party   Area Code
   ☐ Democratic Party   (   )
   ☐ Green Party   **10** Not applicable in this
   ☐ Libertarian Party   County
   ☐ Peace and Freedom Party
   ☐ Republican Party
   ☐ Decline to State
   ☐ Other (Specify) _____

11 HAVE YOU EVER BEEN REGISTERED TO VOTE? Yes☐ No☐
If yes, complete this section to the best of your knowledge concerning your **most recent** registration.

   Name (as registered)

   Former Address

   City   County   State

   Political Party

READ THIS STATEMENT AND WARNING PRIOR TO SIGNING
I am a citizen of the United States and will be at least 18 years of age at the time of the next election. I am not imprisoned or on parole for the conviction of a felony. I certify under **penalty of perjury** under the laws of the State of California that the information on this affidavit is true and correct.
WARNING
Perjury is punishable by imprisonment in state prison for two, three or four years. §126 Penal Code

12 SIGNATURE — Sign on line in box below.

►

► Date   **59 AD 609000**

13 If someone helps fill out or keeps this form, see #13 instructions below. (   )

___ ___ ___

SAMPLE

VOCABULARY: Find the Meaning

On the line write the word or phrase that best completes each sentence.

1. People vote in _____ to choose leaders.

   campaigns   elections   opinions

2. The people who are trying to get elected are the _____ .

   employers   citizens   candidates

3. A _____ is the place where you go to vote.

ballot   polling place   court

4. The form that lists the candidates is called a _____.

poll   opinion   ballot

5. All the ways a candidate seeks support to win an election are called the

_____ .

campaign   political party   volunteer work

COMPREHENSION: Finish the Paragraph

Use the following words or phrases to finish the paragraph.
Write the words you choose on the correct lines.

citizen
speeches
news reports
government
Constitution
register
political party
race
opinions

To vote in elections, you have to be an American _____ . The _____ protects your right to vote. You cannot lose your right to vote because of your sex, _____ , or religion. Before you can vote, you have to _____ . When you register, you can become a member of a _____ . You can get information about the candidates from _____ and _____ .

Learn the difference between facts and _____ about the candidates. By using your right to vote, you have a voice in the

_____ .

Thinking and Writing

Each year on Election Day, many people do not vote. Do you think it is important for every citizen to register and vote? In your journal explain why or why not.

A

affidavit A legal form. page 116

Aid to Families with Dependent Children (AFDC) A program that provides money to low-income families with children. page 101

ambulance A van that is used to take a sick or injured person to the hospital. page 69

ammonia A liquid with a strong smell that is used for cleaning. page 60

appliances Machines that do certain jobs. A stove is an appliance that cooks food. page 33

attractive Looking pretty or nice. page 33

available Ready. An available apartment is one that can be rented. page 18

B

baking soda A white powder that is sometimes used for baking cakes and cookies. It is also used for cleaning. It kills odors. page 59

ballot A form used for voting. page 115

birth certificate A paper from a local government that has information about a person's name, birth, and parents. page 101

borax A white powder that is used for cleaning. Borax kills germs. page 59

boric acid A poisonous powder that kills cockroaches. Sometimes it is colored so that you will not think it is baking soda. page 63

bulletin boards Boards on which ads and notices are hung. page 17

burglar A person who enters the homes and businesses of others in order to steal. page 91

burglar alarm An appliance that makes a loud ringing noise if someone tries to break into a home. page 95

burglarized When someone has broken into a home or business to steal. page 90

C

campaign All the ways a candidate seeks support to win an election. page 114

candidate A person who is trying to get elected to a job in government. page 112

carbohydrates A nutrient that gives the body energy. page 49

chlorine bleach A part of many cleansers. It is also used to make laundry whiter. page 60

cholesterol A fatty substance in the blood. Too much cholesterol in the blood can cause heart disease. page 49

citizens People who are members of a nation and have the rights of that nation. page 103

classified ads Lists in the newspaper for jobs, used products, and housing. These ads are placed in a separate section of the newspaper. page 10

crime An act, like murder, that is against the law. page 90

D

deadbolt A type of lock that offers good protection against burglars. page 94

Democratic Party One of the two largest American political parties. page 113

Department of Housing and Urban Development (HUD) A federal government agency that helps people with low incomes find housing that they can afford. page 105

department of social services A state agency that helps people get many kinds of services. page 105

deposit Money that you give the landlord when you rent a home. The deposit shows that you plan to pay your rent each month. page 7

detergent Soap that can be used for cleaning clothes and items in the home. page 80

disability A problem that makes a person less able to do certain things. If you have a hearing disability, then you do not hear very well. page 9

discount store A large store with low prices. page 40

discrimination Treating people unfairly because of their age, race, sex, religion, or disability. page 19

dispatcher The telephone operator who sends help. page 74

down payment The money you pay in order to get a mortgage. The down payment pays part of the cost of a home. page 6

drowsiness Feeling sleepy. page 79

E

efficiency apartment A one-room apartment with a bathroom and a small kitchen. page 8

election An event in which people choose leaders by voting. page 110

emergency A dangerous time that needs to be handled quickly and correctly. Often outside help is needed to handle a home emergency. page 68

employment information Information about where you work and the kind of job you do. page 30

EMS Emergency Medical Services. You call EMS when you need emergency help. page 74

energy The strength to work or do other things. page 49

engraving pen A tool that can make marks on plastic and metal. The marks cannot be removed easily. page 92

evacuate To leave your home. page 73

expiration date A date printed on a product. This is the last date a product should be bought or used. page 53

F

fee Money that is charged for a service. page 17

fiber A carbohydrate from plants that helps the body remove wastes. page 49

fire extinguisher A container filled with chemicals. When these chemicals are sprayed on a fire, the fire is put out. page 71

flatware Forks, knives, and spoons. page 41

Food and Drug Administration (FDA) A federal agency that checks the safety of foods, medicines, and make-up. page 104

food processor A small appliance that can chop, grind, stir, and mix foods. page 40

fumes The gases given off by products like paint and nail polish. page 80

fuse A safety wire that melts and shuts off the electricity when too much electricity is used at one time. page 83

H

homicide The killing of one person by another person. page 91

housing The different kinds of homes people live in. page 5

hurricane A dangerous storm with heavy rains and strong winds. page 72

I

Immigration and Naturalization Services (INS) A federal agency that helps people from other nations get legal papers to live in the United States. It also helps people become American citizens. page 103

income All the money you earn from your job and from interest on your savings. page 10

insecticide A poisonous product that is used to kill insects. Many insecticides come in spray cans. page 63

L

landlord The person who owns your home and collects your rent. page 7

lease A paper that a tenant signs when renting an apartment. A lease tells the amount of rent and the rules for living in the apartment. page 20

M

maiden name A woman's last name when she was born. page 106

managers People who take care of a group home. page 9

Medicaid A program to help people with low incomes pay for medical care. page 101

minerals Nutrients that are needed by the body to provide healthy teeth, muscles, bones, and blood cells. page 49

mortgage The money that you borrow in order to buy a house. Mortgage money can be paid back over a period of many years. page 6

N

natural disaster An accident caused by nature. page 72

non-stick coating A special seal that keeps food from sticking to the inside of a pot. page 41

nutrients Substances in food that the body needs for health and life. The six nutrients you need are carbohydrates, proteins, fats, vitamins, minerals, and water. page 49

O

operator A worker who answers the phone. page 70

opinion A belief that tells how you think or feel about a person or event. page 114

overdose Taking too much of a medicine. page 85

P

peephole A small hole in a door. It allows you to see outside without opening the door. page 94

perjury Swearing to something that is not true. Perjury is against the law. page 116

pickproof Cannot be picked open. A pickproof lock is a lock that needs to be opened with a key. page 94

poisonous Able to make a living person or thing to become sick or die. page 60

political party A large group of people who have similar beliefs about government. This group tries to get members of their party elected. page 113

polling place The place where you vote. page 115

pollution Dirt, chemicals, and wastes in the air and water. page 59

poultry Birds like chickens, turkeys, and ducks that are used for food. page 53

power failure A time when there is no electricity. All electric lights and appliances stop working. page 73

primary election An election in which members of a political party elect their candidates for the main election. page 114

property taxes The taxes you pay to the government on your home and your land. page 6

proteins Nutrients that the body uses for growth and repair. page 49

R

real estate agent A person who sells and rents houses and apartments. page 17

receipt A paper that proves you gave money to someone to pay for something. page 21

recipes Directions for cooking or baking foods. page 43

renew To make new again. To renew a lease means to get a new lease when the old lease ends. page 20

Republican Party One of the two largest American political parties. page 113

S

sexual assault A crime in which an attacker uses force to perform sexual acts on another person. page 91

smoke detector A small machine that beeps when there is smoke in a room or hallway. page 71

state employment agency A state agency that can help a person find a job. page 102

superintendent A person who manages and cares for an apartment building. page 17

T

tenant A person who pays rent to live in a house or an apartment. page 18

thermometer A small appliance that measures temperature. page 39

thermostat A small appliance that controls the temperature of an oven, freezer, or refrigerator. page 39

thrift shops Stores where you can buy good used clothing and other products for a low price. page 33

tornado A kind of windstorm shaped like a funnel. page 72

U

unconscious When someone has passed out or fainted. page 69

unemployment insurance If you lose your job, this state program may pay part of your salary while you look for work. page 102

utensils Tools used for preparing and storing food. page 41

utilities Services to your home such as water, electricity, gas, and telephone. page 7

V

vital records office A government office that keeps birth and death certificates. page 106

vitamins A group of nutrients that the body needs in small amounts in order to work and grow well. page 49

volunteer work Work that people are not paid to do. page 113

W

warranty A company's promise to repair or replace a product if it does not work right. page 40

washing soda A white powder that can be used for washing clothes. It can be used for cleaning floors, walls, and bathrooms. page 59

workers' compensation A state program that may pay part of your salary and medical bills if you get hurt or sick while working. page 102

INDEX

ANSWER KEY

Chapter 1

Page 12 Workshop

1. gas; electricity
2. efficiency
3. furnished
4. 2 bedrooms; 1 bathroom
5. Smith Realty
6. Redwood
7. Answers will vary.

Page 14 Workshop Practice

Unfurnished apartment in Lakeview. Large 3 bedrooms, 2 bathrooms, dining room, new wall-to-wall carpeting, dishwasher, new refrigerator, washer and dryer in kitchen, air conditioning, gas included, good location near bus, deposit required. $490 a month. Call 432-9926.

Pages 14–15 Vocabulary

1. mortgage
2. income
3. deposit
4. efficiency apartments
5. property

Page 15 Comprehension

1. True
2. False; You pay your landlord a deposit when you rent a home.
3. False; You have to pay for home repairs and utilities when you own your own home.
4. True
5. True

Chapter 2

Page 22 Workshop

1. 413 Loyola Avenue
2. 2 years
3. Carmen Sanchez
4. New Orleans General Hospital
5. 2 years
6. 0200306562

Page 25 Workshop

7. one
8. AAA OOO
9. sign outside building
10. June 1, 1994
11. 2 years
12. $345

Page 26 Workshop Practice

Answers will vary.

Page 27 Vocabulary

1. c
2. d
3. a
4. b

Page 27 Comprehension

You can get information about available apartments from bulletin boards and the classified ads in the newspaper. Look at an apartment carefully before you rent it. Make sure the apartment building looks clean and safe. The landlord will ask you questions before renting the apartment to you. If the landlord feels you will be a good tenant, you will be given a lease that tells how much rent you pay.

Chapter 3

Page 34 Workshop

1. only for Steven
2. 2/10/94
3. 52 Central Avenue, #4L Nashville, TN 37206
4. 599 Post Road, #2B Richmond, VA 23220
5. 7 days

Page 36 Workshop Practice

Check number 1 for individual or entire family. Fill in number 2 with a date in 3 weeks. Use today's date for number 9.

Pages 36–37 Comprehension

1. You may need to clean and paint. You may need to cover the windows.
2. Utility companies want to know your new address, the address and phone number of your job, another phone number where you can be reached, and the date to start service.
3. You need light bulbs, lamp, soap, toilet paper, food, towels, bedding, broom, and chairs.

4. You can buy furniture on sale or used furniture in thrift shops and at garage sales. You can also check the classified ads.
5. Answers will vary.

Page 37 Vocabulary
Answers will vary. You may use more than one vocabulary word in a sentence.

Chapter 4
Page 44 Workshop
1. limited
2. 5 years
3. date of purchase
4. service trips, improper installation, replacement of house fuses or resetting of circuit breakers, improper usage, damage caused by accidents

Page 46 Workshop Practice
Answers will vary. You should include that you would have saved your sales slip or canceled check. You would look in the telephone book for the place to take the oven to have it fixed.

Pages 46–47 Comprehension
1. thermometer
2. electric mixer
3. You can use less fat.
4. one or two days
5. as soon as the oven is cool

Page 47 Vocabulary
1. thermostat
2. food processor
3. utensils
4. warranty
5. flatware
6. recipe

Chapter 5
Page 55 Workshop
(in any order)
Very Healthy Choices
1. apple
2. banana
3. canned tuna in water
4. carrot sticks
5. fruit juice
6. grapes
7. lean turkey breast
8. low-fat cheese
9. nonfat cakes and cookies
10. oatmeal
11. orange
12. plain baked potato
13. salad
14. skim milk
15. skinless chicken breast
16. steamed vegetables
17. unbuttered popcorn
18. unsalted pretzels
19. watermelon
20. whole-wheat bread

Less Healthy Choices
1. bacon
2. butter
3. candy bars
4. canned tuna in oil
5. chocolate chip cookies
6. corn chips
7. donuts
8. egg yolks
9. French fries
10. fried chicken
11. fried foods
12. frosted cakes
13. hot dogs
14. ice cream
15. marshmallows
16. potato chips
17. salami
18. salted peanuts
19. sour cream
20. sweet cereal

Page 56 Workshop Practice
Answers will vary.

Pages 56–57 Comprehension
1. Your body needs carbohydrates, proteins, fats, vitamins, minerals, and water.
2. Fatty foods can cause cholesterol to build up in the blood. Too much cholesterol can cause heart disease.
3. A healthy diet comes mostly from the bread, vegetable, and fruit groups.
4. Any two of the following are correct:
   — Cook eggs, fish, all meat, chicken, and turkey completely and at the right temperature.
   — Wash knives, cutting board, and counter after you prepare poultry.
   — Rinse poultry before cooking, and pat dry with a paper towel.
   — Never use foods in dented, leaking, swollen, or rusty cans.
   — Never eat moldy food.
5. Food in cans that are dented, leaking, swollen, or rusty may cause food poisoning.

Page 57 Vocabulary
1. c
2. e
3. a
4. b
5. d

Chapter 6
Page 65 Workshop
1. 1 cup per load or 1 tbsp. per gallon
2. Dilute bleach with 1 qt. of water first.
3. no
4. 1/8 cup
5. no
6. Give 1 or 2 glasses of milk or water. Call a doctor or Poison Control Center.
7. Mixing may cause dangerous gases.

Page 66 Workshop Practice
1. 1/2 cup
2. no
3. Flush with water.
4. open

Pages 66–67 Vocabulary
1. chlorine bleach
2. pollution
3. baking soda
4. boric acid
5. poisonous

Page 67 Comprehension
1. False; Chemicals used in cleansers are poisonous.
2. False; It is not safe to mix ammonia with chlorine bleach.
3. True
4. True
5. False; Mouse poisons and insecticides are not safe for children, adults, and pets.

Chapter 7
Page 74 Workshop
1. 911
2. 244–2000
3. 1–800–342–1000
4. Dr. Alicia Smith
5. Community Hospital
6. 555–3940
7. 753–6112
8. 762–1500

Page 76 Workshop Practice
Answers will vary.

Page 77 Vocabulary
Answers will vary. You may use more than one vocabulary word in a sentence.

Page 77 Comprehension
1. flashlight, candles, matches, battery radio, blankets, first-aid kit
2. once a month
3. baking soda
4. Call the gas company from your neighbor's phone.

Chapter 8
Page 85 Workshop
1. anyone who has asthma, glaucoma, emphysema, chronic pulmonary disease, shortness of breath, difficulty in breathing or difficulty in urination due to enlargement of the prostate gland
2. excitability, especially in children; drowsiness
3. driving a motor vehicle or operating machinery or drinking alcoholic beverages

4. seek professional assistance or contact a Poison Control Center immediately

Page 86 Workshop Practice
1. It can cause eye and skin irritation on contact. It may cause respiratory tract irritation if inhaled or be harmful if swallowed.
2. Flush immediately with large amounts of water, especially under eyelids.
3. Move to fresh air or seek medical attention if trouble continues.

Pages 86–87 Vocabulary
1. drowsiness
2. unconscious
3. detergents
4. fumes
5. fuse

Page 87 Comprehension
1. True
2. True
3. False; It is dangerous to wear headphones when riding a bike.
4. True
5. False; Keep your windows open when using paint and paint thinners.

Page 89 Crossword Puzzle

Chapter 9
Page 97 Workshop
1. A Neighborhood Crime Watch helps reduce crime. It helps people find out how to make their homes safe.

2. The block captain is the contact with the police. The police give the block captain information about crime prevention. The block captain gives the information to the group.
3. The police teach members how to make their homes safer. Members learn how to prevent attacks.

Page 98 Workshop Practice
1. I could call the police and get information about the program.
2. Then I would talk to my neighbors about the program.
3. I would organize a block meeting, and we would elect a block captain. The block captain would work with the police on how to get started. The block captain would report back to us.
4. Then the police would meet with us as a group. They would teach us how to make our homes safer and how to prevent attacks.
5. As members of the group, we would look out for one another. We would call police if we saw a stranger hanging around the neighborhood.
6. If we had enough members, we could buy a Crime Watch sign to put up in the neighborhood.

Page 99 Vocabulary
1. Crimes
2. homicide
3. sexual assault
4. deadbolt lock

Page 99 Comprehension
To protect yourself and your home, you need to try to keep <u>strangers</u> out of your home. Never open your door without looking through the <u>peephole</u>. Never leave your <u>key</u> under a doormat. When leaving your home, always lock all doors and <u>windows</u>. Have locks for your doors that are <u>pickproof</u>. Report all crimes to the <u>police</u> at once.

Chapter 10
Pages 106–107 Workshop
1. to get a passport
2. Pulaski County
3. Butler
4. $5.00

Page 108 Workshop Practice
Answers will vary. Be sure to include all the information in your letter. You can look in the phone book or check in the library to find the address of the vital records office that you need.

Pages 108–109 Comprehension
1. True
2. False; Local governments keep records of births, deaths, marriages, and divorces.
3. True
4. True
5. False; The federal government has an agency to make sure new medicines are safe.

Page 109 Vocabulary
1. Medicaid
2. state employment agency
3. citizens
4. workers' compensation
5. Department of Housing and Urban Development
6. Food and Drug Administration

Chapter 11
Pages 116–117 Workshop
1. Los Angeles County
2. Democratic
3. yes
4. 403 Prairie Avenue, Los Angeles
5. yes
6. Tim Collins

Page 118 Workshop Practice
The answers on the form will vary. Print clearly and fill out the form completely.

Pages 118–119 Vocabulary
1. elections
2. candidates
3. polling place
4. ballot
5. campaign

Page 119 Comprehension
To vote in elections, you have to be an American <u>citizen</u>. The <u>Constitution</u> protects your right to vote. You cannot lose your right to vote because of your sex, <u>race</u>, or religion. Before you can vote, you have to <u>register</u>. When you register, you can become a member of a <u>political party</u>. You can get information about the candidates from <u>speeches</u> and <u>news reports</u>. Learn the difference between facts and <u>opinions</u> about the candidates. By using your right to vote, you have a voice in the <u>government</u>.